Vonu: A Strategy for Self-Liberation

By: Shane Radliff

liberty under attack publications

Copyleft Notice

This book is covered by a BipCot NoGovernment License. Re-use and modification is permitted to anyone EXCEPT for governments and the bludgies thereof.

Disclaimer

The purpose of this book is to provide individuals with potential solutions in increasing their personal freedom. Many of these solutions are perfectly legal, some are in a gray area, but some are outright illegal. That said, neither the author nor the publisher recommend or advocate anyone break the law. If you decide to pursue any solutions presented in this book, it is done at your own risk and of your own accord. In other words, be smart and practice excellent security culture.

It should also be noted that nothing herein should be construed as legal advice. The author is not a lawyer, nor does he play one on TV. Do your own legal research or consult a professional.

LIBERTY UNDER ATTACK PUBLICATIONS *tell your story*

1. **An Illusive Phantom of Hope: A Critique of Reformism** by Kyle Rearden (Audiobook/Anthology)
2. **The Production of Security** by Gustave de Molinari (Audiobook)
3. **Are Cops Constitutional?** by Roger Roots (Audiobook)
4. **Argumentation Ethics: An Anthology** by Hans-Herman Hoppe et al (Anthology)
5. **Just Below The Surface: A Guide to Security Culture** by Kyle Rearden (Audiobook/Paperback)
6. **Sedition, Subversion, and Sabotage, Field Manual No. 1: A Three Part Solution to the State** by Ben Stone (Paperback/Audiobook)
7. **#agora** by anonymous (Paperback/Audiobook)
8. **Vonu: A Strategy for Self-Liberation** by Shane Radliff (Paperback)
9. **Second Realm: Book on Strategy** by Smuggler and XYZ (Paperback/Audiobook)
10. **Vonu: The Search for Personal Freedom** by Rayo (Special Paperback Reprint/Audiobook)
11. **Vonu: The Search for Personal Freedom, Part 2 [Letters From Rayo]** (Paperback)
12. **Going Mobile** by Tom Marshall (Paperback/Audiobook)
13. **Anarchist to Abolitionist: A Bad Quaker's Journey** by Ben Stone
14. **Brushfire, A Thriller** by Matthew Wojtecki (Paperback/Audiobook)
15. **2048 (A BRUSHFIRE THRILLER)** by Matthew Wojtecki
16. **VonuLife, March 1973** by Rayo et al (Paperback)
17. **Ocean Freedom Notes** by Jim Stumm, Rayo, et al (Paperback)
18. **The Big Book of Secret Hiding Places** by Jack Luger (Paperback)
19. **The Invention of Evil** by Henry Jones (Paperback/Kindle)
20. **Low Cost Living Notes** by Jim Stumm et al (Paperback/Kindle)
21. **Survival Gardening Notes** by Jim Stumm et al (Paperback/Kindle)
22. **The Permanent Floating Voluntary Society** by Kerry Thornley (Paperback/Kindle)
23. **A Vonu Guide to Firearms** by Josiah Warren & Shane Radliff (Paperback)

Visit <u>LibertyUnderAttack.com</u> for discounted bundles, privacy tools, and more!

Dedication

TO RAYO, who walked this path before any of us thought of it, and to the freedom pioneers carving niches of personal autonomy in a world opposed to it.

Table of Contents

Foreword

Since I first became an activist almost four decades ago, I have watched "liberty" trends come and go; all while the State grows in size and strength. I have seen the fruit of the labor of good people be taken, misdirected, and usurped, all in the name of liberty. I have observed dedicated, freedom-minded folks deceived, fooled, and robbed under the guise of liberty. Despite the intentions, these good honest people were inadvertently advancing the cause of the State by supporting systems that underpin the Colossus.

I have watched political deceivers who have learned that a few well-chosen words will act as dog whistles, and otherwise smart people will abandon reason and logic as they cling to a politician as if he were their favorite uncle. I have watched as libertarians and others, faithfully believed the lies of politicians and would-be politicians who promised to roll back the abuses of government or restrain the advance of government.

I watched the most successful of those politicians get wealthy, embed their family members in government or party positions, and retire without shrinking government by a single penny. And as expected: government grew, spending skyrocketed, national debts exploded, and yet more liberties were lost.

Currently, there is a deafening noise from the cheers surrounding the YouTube libertarian cybervangelists, only surpassed by the unjustified reverence, awe, and blind dedication. These holy elders of liberty can only be spoken of in praise, lest their faithful minions rain Internet hate upon you for your blasphemies. Yet the best advice these cybervangelists and holy liberty elders can offer the freedom-minded individual is "vote for me," "beg government to be nice," "beg government to slightly lower spending," and "beg government to audit the Fed."

Like Emmanuel Goldstein guiding The Brotherhood in controlled opposition to Big Brother, those most revered in the so called Liberty Movement are simply encouraging their followers to continue doing the same thing that has never worked. Namely, using the immorality and aggression of government, to make the immorality and aggression of government somehow less immoral and less aggressive. It could pass as a hilarious sketch comedy if it weren't happening in real time around us every single day.

On the other hand, something I've rarely witnessed is the freedom pioneer who is able to sidestep the personality cults, the con-artists, and the windbags, while sifting through the mountains of "liberty" publications to find the hidden jewels of truth left by the often forgotten or unsung visionaries who came before us.

I am speaking of that rare individual who can see that doing the same thing generation after generation is not a wise course and will never lead to freedom.

I am speaking of the few today who have made the conscious choice to abandon collectivist solutions, abandon faith in a liberty champion, and personally embrace vonu & self-liberation aimed at using the liberties we currently have to become as free as possible, as soon as possible.

In the process of compiling ***Vonu: A Strategy for Self-Liberation***, Shane has dug through mountains of out-of-print material and works almost lost to history. He, along with a small group of co-conspirators, have resurrected a genre of the freedom movement that had all but vanished.

Shane's timing in delivering this book could not have been better. Without the baggage of the so called Liberty Movement, waves of people are seeking greater freedom by embracing minimalist lifestyles in a variety of ways. From the tiny house movement, festival circuits, van nomadism, and even the RV lifestyle, people of every age and income classification are taking direct action in their lives in an attempt to free themselves from the traps of modern consumerism and the chains of the State.

People are tired of simply drudging through traffic in a daily commute only to waste hours of their lives banging at a virtual feed bar in the virtual cage that we call a cubical. As the bosses bark out orders, we all know deep inside, the only reward we will see is more debt and the occasional upgrade to an overpriced phone.

That is, unless we do something about it. Unless we act!

Many people have also come to this same conclusion. Their problem is in knowing what to do that will directly lead them to the freedom they desire. No thinking person wants to continue doing the same thing over and over while hoping for a different result. But few people have the time and resources to research such a wide topic.

What Shane provides for us in ***Vonu: A Strategy for Self-Liberation*** is refined information that will be extremely helpful in the decision-making process for anyone seeking the next step in freeing themselves from this self-inflicted bondage called modern society. Those in the gaming world could refer to Shane's book as a set of cheat codes or perhaps a walk-through, designed to show the reader a path through a wide wilderness of choices, on the way to achieving a life as close to true freedom as possible today.

You could spend the next forty years of your life chasing dreams, giving your hard-earned cash to liberty cheerleaders, or convincing yourself that some politician is going to magically make government produce freedom. Or you can cut through the hogwash and empty promises and take the actions needed to live as free a life as you can as soon as possible.

I choose to stop talking, stop wishing, and stop following. I choose action.

Ben Stone
April 2018
Bad Quaker Podcast

Definitions

1. **Vonu**: the condition or quality of, as well as the action of achieving, an invulnerability to coercion.
2. **Vonuer**: having comparatively more an invulnerability to coercion.
3. **Vonuence**: in the process of achieving an invulnerability to coercion.
4. **Vonuan**: one who has an invulnerability to coercion.
5. **Vonuist**: one who advocates for an invulnerability to coercion.
6. **Vonuism**: the advocacy of an invulnerability to coercion.
7. **Vonuum**: the place or situation of an invulnerability to coercion.
8. **Vonumy**: the art of achieving an invulnerability to coercion.
9. **Vonumer**: one skilled at an invulnerability to coercion.
10. **Political Crusading**: a strategy to restore liberty by working inside of the system in order to change it from within. Examples of this are petitioning, writing to congressmen, protesting, grassroots lobbying, running for public office, and voting. Synonyms include reformism and bullshit libertarianism.
11. **Security Culture**: the direct application of the right to privacy. As a strategy to maintain liberty, it is focused on the *how* of making privacy happen in the real world, given that the philosophical justification for privacy is self-evident, particularly through argumentation ethics.
12. **Agorism**: a libertarian strategy that seeks to abolish the State through grey and black-market activities, thereby developing the capabilities of the agora (an unlicensed, unregulated, untaxed, laissez-faire freed market).
13. **Second Realm**: an updated version of Temporary Autonomous Zones (TAZs). Essentially, the ability to conduct trade and other activities (including vices) in certain areas at particular times without reprisal from the State. TAZs were originally conceived of as geographically mobile, like vonu shelters, yet now it may include cyberspace, such as the deep web.
14. **Controlled Schizophrenia**: the mental state of an opportunistic citizen-serf within the servile society who practices doublethink, yet who still acts in his own best interest. Political crusaders are but just one example of this in action.
15. **Collective Movementism**: an aggregate set of behaviors and actions that are aimed towards large-scale socio-political change in

the furtherance of specific goals. Examples include the environmentalist movement, the alt-right, the labor movement, the libertarian movement, the public lands movement, the anti-war movement, the gay rights movement, the women's' rights movement, and the civil rights movement.

16. **The Servile Society**: a society that does not respect self-ownership or individual liberty, but rather heralds the supremacy of government and authority; in other words, it upholds the collective as superior to the individual. A one-directional isolation of import-export is used to maintain access to the servile society's open-but-not-free trading centers yet denying them access to a vonuan's home through importing goods and knowledge while exporting labor or products back out to the servile society.

17. **Legal Interstices**: grey areas within the law that can be used to violate the spirit of the law while simultaneously keeping the letter of the law.

18. **Mean Time to Harassment**: the strength of vonu, usually expressed in years. MTH is typically used to gauge the profitable viability of concealing a vonuum relative to one's competency at vonumy.

19. **Freemate**: a relationship style wherein the participants contract with each other individually, rather than by way of the State; in other words, such issues are the concern of the people involved, and no one else.

20. **Bludg/bludgie**: a derisive term used by vonuans to describe law enforcers; also called "bluecoats," "police extortionists," "pigs," etc.

Introduction

Back in 2018 when I first published the book you're about to read, I could have never imagined the journey I was about to embark upon. At that time, I had just decided to quit my newly acquired electrician apprenticeship job that I really enjoyed, largely on a whim, and move to Austin, Texas to live with my former *Vonu Podcast* co-host, Kyle Rearden.

So, in the span of a few weeks, the entire trajectory of my life changed. It wasn't planned or even really consciously driven...it's almost as if my True Will was finally going to make its appearance, whether me or anyone else liked it or not.

After a couple months staying with Kyle in a third-story apartment in north Austin, my situation changed again, and even more radically. He informed me that he and his freemate had found a house and were going to move out ahead of the lease expiring, meaning I would have to take over the exorbitantly priced rent plus utilities on my own if I were to stay there.

Needless to say, I sought out other options – rooms to rent on Craigslist, shared housing, cheap options that I could actually afford in the high-priced servile society lifestyle that is Austin.

I shared my situation with some friends on social media and a buddy of mine, Jason Henza, put forth an interesting proposition. At the end of the month, he would be driving through Austin on his way to Acapulco, Mexico, and that I could ride down and stay with him. He was also generous enough to offer to cover some costs for me, since I was in a tumultuous situation financially.

Of course, my first thought was, "Hell no. There's no way that's going to happen."

But then again, I didn't really have any other options...and this is exactly the type of adventure I wanted, exactly the type of adventure I needed.

I made the minimal preparations that I could and scrounged up as much fiat currency as was available in the meantime...thankfully, Austin being the mega-city it is, it was pretty easy to find a few temporary jobs on the weekends (major events like Formula One, business conferences, etc.), in addition to a cheap tent camping spot in Liberty Hill for a few weeks before heading really far south.

Leaving some personal (non-vonu) experiences aside, we arrived safely in Acapulco and I got to enjoy a couple months with a somewhat-large anarchist community, in what truly was a tropical paradise.

In terms of bludgies and other State agents, it is undoubtedly better for a vonuan self-liberator. You're usually just one really cheap bribe away from your freedom, and if you're a Gringo, they are even more likely to leave you alone. It's even a lot easier to acquire legal, authentic Mexican identification too, whether it is a driver's license, registration, etc., enabling prospects for a simplified second identity.

But in terms of private coercion, it really is a dangerous place (though, worth noting, this "private" violence is still essentially State-caused, a result of the War on Drugs – don't forget about the USSA government literally shipping weapons south of the border too).

My time in Acapulco ended in December 2018, but I had planned on returning for the Acapulco conference that February.

About a week before the conference was set to begin, John Galton was killed and Henza was shot multiple times at John and Lily's house high up on the mountain...a place I spent a lot of time at, and likely would have been at if I was still in Mexico with Henza.

I'm extremely thankful Henza and Lily are still here with us to share their powerful stories...and may John rest in peace. He was truly a dedicated freedom pioneer.

After John's death, I settled back in on what is now my homestead in southern Illinois...working at the family distillery, podcasting, and largely, just spending time decompressing alone in the wilderness. This was what I consider the official start to my liberated lifestyle, a lifestyle wherein my time is my own and I am free to follow my passions.

I made some critical lifestyle changes, such as quitting alcohol and adopting a new, much healthier way-of-eating, and gained a whole new take on life. The brain fog was entirely gone, I felt amazing, and I discovered my newfound, front-running passion: learning about health, the miraculous human body, and investigating health modalities to assist individuals in restoring balance in their bodies (i.e. "reversing disease").

But of course, as per the connected nature of this realm, this rabbit hole of health led to the topics of breakthrough "free" energy, the **P.A.Z.NIA Department of Health & Wellness** (of which now has an authentic Rife machine, one of George Wiseman's AquaCure machines, & other amazing supplements/tools)…

And in September 2020, **The Free Republic of P.A.Z.NIA** was created; a decentralized network of Second Realms, our own parallel society.

My wonderful freewife and I are nearing food self-sufficiency, our flock currently including: ~12 lambs, a few goats, 30 or 40 birds (chickens, ducks, and turkeys), a half dozen rabbits, a few flourishing gardens, and yearly gatherings of liberation for vetted, traveling van nomads/vonuans.

It's been a helluva handful of years, but I've accomplished the major objective I set out to achieve when I first started digging into solutions way back in 2015: get out of the 9-5 rat race jobs that were literally killing me.

Of course, I've got much bigger dreams (living on a sailboat, the eventual acquisition of a decommissioned aircraft carrier for Second Realm purposes, a complete spagyrics/alchemy laboratory, etc.), but I'm eternally grateful to be where I am, and for all of those who have played a part.

With the recent release of the audiobook, I have decided to release this second edition, with the entirety of the main content remaining the same. I've added this introduction and an additional chapter at the end with more information, since my experiences are so much greater now. Doing it in this manner means that the audiobook can remain as is, and this additional material tacked on later. Big thanks to Fenix Aurora and Matthew Workman for their efforts on this.

I'll leave it there for now and let the 2018 version of my Self walk you through the most liberating freedom strategy I've ever come across. I wish you the best in your pursuit of freedom, and please do reach out if there's any way I can be of service.

Always remember, vonu is yours for the making and the Second Realm is yours for the building.

Cheers from *The Free Republic!*

Shane/Rayo2
August 2022
The Vonu Podcast

Section I: The Philosophy of Vonu

"The basic principle which leads a libertarian from statism to a free society is the same that the founders of libertarianism used to discover the theory itself. That principle is consistency." –Samuel Edward Konkin III, *New Libertarian Manifesto*

Chapter 1: Vonu, A Brief History, & Introduction

Since humans have existed on this Earth, coercion has been used to control, manipulate, and exploit individuals. It is an unfortunate fact of history. The State uses it to keep their hapless citizenry in line and private criminals use it to violate the autonomy of their subjects for personal gain.

So then, what is politics? Politics is the **art** and **science** of managing **centralized coercion**, plain and simple. That being the case, it's no surprise that politics is undoubtedly a counter-intuitive way to decrease the amount of coercion in your life. Would you drink a fifth of Jack Daniels to cure your alcoholism? Engage a couple more prostitutes to assist you in overcoming your sex addiction? What about making a few more trips to Vegas as the means for eradicating that dreaded gambling vice?

As ridiculous as those may sound, using politics to alleviate coercion is a far more dangerous utilization of this failed logic. It has more far-reaching, unintended (and intended) consequences. People's livelihoods have been and can be destroyed by so-called public policy; the State being the apparatus it is, mass murder (i.e. democide), the most deadly form of coercion, is always on the table.

Thus, the problem that freedom pioneers face is coercion.

Back in the 1960s, a man named Tom Marshall ("Rayo") resided in Southern California, then a bustling libertarian community. He was a tech-y engineer, a socially-awkward fellow, a marijuana smoker, not much of a philosopher, but a freedom-seeking libertarian nonetheless. Early on, he spent some time at the Nathaniel Branden Institute, a school teaching the Objectivist philosophy laid out by Ayn Rand (well, at its core, first by Aristotle), until his first major venture came about: the Free Isles Project.

The Free Isles Project spawned out of the Preform-Inform zine. The goal was to conduct research on the efficacy of setting up a new libertarian nation and the seemingly endless possibilities for freedom if it were to come into fruition. Rayo said:

"The "free isle" resident would (hypothetically) have all of the advantages of participating in world commerce while being free from taxes and regulations. Furthermore, a "free isle", if it were successful, could be a very effective demonstration of the merits of laissez-faire capitalism."

Unfortunately (or, fortunately?), it was never successful; hell, it never got past the talking stage. Eventually, the movement subsided after disagreements arose regarding the size and scope of government, the lack of individuals willing to become involved, and the potential ramifications from existing nation states. (As an aside, the latter two are still big problems for libertarian country-building projects today. Thankfully, most of the newer projects are more anarchistic, but the facilitators are often terrible strategists and tacticians – generally, they fail to learn from history.)

Rayo, frustrated with the "all talk, no action" libertarians of his day said "Screw it!" and moved out of his apartment into a camper mounted on his pickup truck: he became a van nomad and began laying the foundation for the most interesting, plausible freedom strategy today.

Naturally though, "freedom" means many different things to different people. "Freedom" to a propertarian anarchist means private property, personal autonomy, and peace; "freedom" to a leftist means "free" healthcare, "free" college, and a massive welfare state; "freedom" to a conservative means "Christianity" (it's not really Christianity; Jesus was most certainly an anarchist), the mass murder known as war, and social(ist) (in)security.

Language is quite fluid, which is why Rayo and Roberta (his freemate) proposed a new term: "Vonu."

"Vonu" is an awkward contraction of the words "**VO**luntary **N**ot v**U**lnerable" and, simply defined, is the condition or quality of, as well as the action of achieving, an invulnerability to coercion. So, with one definition, vonuans avoid the issue of subjective interpretation altogether. You know coercion and violence when you see it; if you make radical lifestyle changes in an attempt to avoid those things, you are a vonuan, as you are taking steps to become more invulnerable to coercion, regardless of whether the perceived threat is "corporations," "the State," or a crime-ridden hellhole.

But, early vonuans also had interesting ways of interpreting "liberty" and "freedom."

"Liberty," as defined by Funk and Wagnall's Standard College Dictionary 1968 (the reference Rayo used in his book), is a measure of freedom within restraints, granted by or through a sovereign power. "Freedom," as defined by the aforementioned source, is the widest term, suggesting complete absence of restraint.

So, vonuans say that liberty is the general exemption from coercion and freedom is an absence of coercion. To gain liberty, one utilizes legal interstices, or, as it is more vernacularly known, legal loopholes within the law. And you know what the State does to those, right? If they can, they close them (damn those gun show loopholes and Ghost Gunners – major props to Cody Wilson).

Rayo specifically had an interesting take on legal interstices. One of his complaints about van nomadism was that it required reliance on "slave tags" (i.e. driver's licensure, registration, mandatory insurance). So, in order to hopefully avoid the coercion of the bludgies, you have a license plate on your car, you hand the bludgie your driver's license, and you keep your tags up-to-date. It's providing a safeguard of sorts, but the "terms and conditions may change" if they "smell" marijuana or if the bludgie in question just wanted to beat you for breathing the wrong way.

Rayo also had a quite negative stance on utopian fantasies like "AnCapistan," a "free world," or a "communist paradise." Therefore, freedom, "the absence of coercion," is a utopian pipedream. Even if the State disappears, there will still be psychopaths, violent murderers, and thieves, hence, there will always be coercion.

He pursued the van nomad lifestyle for quite a while and realized that it wasn't enough for him; he disliked the aforementioned "slave tags" because if you have to ask (and pay off!) the State for permission, are you really free? So, Rayo decided that the wilderness vonu life would offer him the most personal satisfaction and he and Roberta moved into a polyethylene a-tent, deep in the Siskiyou National Forest. He continued to publish a few vonu publications (Preform-Inform, Innovator, VonuLife) and wrote for others, such as Libertarian Connection, the Eleutherian Forum, and Going Mobile, nestled up in his foam hut, under his makeshift tent.

His frustration with libertarians and the community at-large increased and all he saw around him were controlled schizophrenic, political crusaders (see below). He once longed for vonu associations (i.e. van nomad mobile communities, agoras), but his inclination to work with others waned like a recent full moon. As I receive more vonu publications from his time, I hope to find out what truly happened; at this time, all I have is suspicion.

He began to pursue troglodyte living and practiced building underground structures, when he mysteriously ceased communication and disappeared. All that remains is a portion of a letter he wrote to his correspondent (I THINK Jon Fisher, the editor of his first book) dated February 14, 1974:

"My thinking has undergone major changes in the last several months on interfacing, 'alternate economics,' interrelations in general...I, too, am becoming very dubious as to the value of all 'libertarian club' involvements...We do not intend to use the 'libertarian club' in the future as an avenue for gaining non-anonymous friends or associates."

But, the strategy he and other freedom seekers pioneered is still just as efficacious as it was before, and even more so thanks to advancements in technology.

So, how does vonu differ from direct action more generally, such as the methods listed on *The Freedom Umbrella of Direct Action* (FUDA)?

Well, with many of the strategies on the FUDA, you can more-or-less continue living the same lifestyle you did before (i.e. a 9-5 job in the servile society, paying some taxes, etc.) and receive **some** increases in your personal freedom.

Vonu, on the otherhand, is a lifestyle change – it is a reorganization of your entire life, but the increase in personal freedom is quite substantial (and that's putting it mildly). Examples of these vonu lifestyles include: van nomadism and wilderness vonu (both strategies Rayo and Roberta utilized), minimalist sailboating, intentional communities (mobile or stationary), vonuing in cities, perpetual traveling, and utilizing ethical enclaves. I'll discuss all of these in substantial depth below, but first, let's take a look at the few honorable mentions of vonu by other libertarians.

Chapter 2: Rayo's Influence on the Libertarian & Anarchist Communities

As should be evident, Rayo's work was basically forgotten until Kyle Rearden and I launched The Vonu Podcast in January of 2017, but Rayo likely influenced a significant, popular strategy within anarchist circles: agorism.

In INNOVATOR, November 1965, Rayo wrote an article titled, Self-Seeking: Ethical Enclave (Black Markets). He defines an ethical enclave as:

"voluntary transactions between individuals who are living under a collectivist government, when such transactions are conducted independent of that government. "Ethical" denotes the distinguishing characteristic of the participating individuals: an adherence to the ethical principle of voluntarism, the principle that no one should initiate violence or threat of violence against another. And "enclave" denotes physical emersion within a philosophically alien society. An ethical enclave is not necessarily a separate geographical entity."

So, Rayo was an early voluntaryist (before the term was re-appropriated, even) and he was describing what would be more vernacularly known as an "agora." He continues:

"An ethical enclave, by existing within the territorial domain of a coercive government is either legal – utilizing "interstices" in the taxes and regulations of that government, or illegal – operating despite threats of violence."

Now he's describing the black and grey markets of agorism – either trading in goods and services that aren't illegal, or dealing outright contraband. But, he doesn't stop there. What are the differences between ethical enclave entrepreneurs and black market operators? He says that "the differences are significant."

"The mixed premise "black market" operator, while violating socialist laws, still holds (at least subconsciously) some of the premises embodied in laws. He may experience a depressing sense of guilt; he may act with the handicap of psychological conflicts. The enclave entrepreneur, however, disavows not only the particular instance of initiated violence but the collectivist morality as well. He experiences an exhilarating sense of righteousness; he acts with the confidence and certitude of psychological consistency.

The enclave entrepreneur, furthermore, is dealing not only with immoral (by their own definition) "criminals" but with producers – with moral individuals who are committed on principle to hold confidences and honor contracts. His "costs of doing business" therefore tend to be less."

In other words, he's calling your typical black market operator a controlled schizophrenic (see below). The ethical enclave operator has "an exhilarating sense of righteousness," as he recognizes the attempted violations of his autonomy, and his act of rebellion in restoring it.

Furthermore, he discusses the significance of dealing peer-to-peer with like-minded individuals. Thankfully, this is the direction things have been going for about 20 years with open-source technology. Rayo was just, as always, way ahead of the curve.

Recall the agorist notion of "starve the State, then smash it." Even though ethical enclaves are: 1) just an option for vonuans, not a requirement, and 2) small-scale focused with no goal of abolition (vonuans are "satisfied to co-exist in protracted conflict with the State"), Rayo still believed black and grey market trading could be a thorn in the State's side:

"Ethical enclave trading profits participating individuals and promotes liberty in general by reducing the plunder available to the collectivist government – plunder which would most probably be used to finance further violations of liberty, plus propaganda to rationalize the violations. The potential effect of ethical enclave trading should not be underestimated. Mixed socialist government direct most of their extortions and regulations at trade – they tax primarily income and sales. But a transaction can easily be taxed only with the cooperation of at least one party to the transaction. **Large scale non-cooperation would render income and sales taxes ineffective and greatly reduce government revenues – an ultimate check on a State's capability for violence against its subjects.**

An ethical enclave would also encourage growth of a "libertarian movement" by adding self-interest motivations." [**Emphasis added**]

So, it sure as hell sounds almost identical to the strategy Sam Konkin (SEK3) proposed. The last question to answer is, "Was Konkin familiar with Rayo/vonu?"

The answer? Yes. Undoubtedly. The following four excerpts are from articles published in the Southern Libertarian Review, January-June 1975, all authored by Konkin (all of which you can find online):

1) "Anarchozionism"

"The Preform crowd either Browned out or went into escapist trips such as becoming nomads, troglodytes, or wilderness dwellers. They sought 'invulnerability to coercion'—or vonu—and PREFORM-INFORM became Vonulife. Recently it sputtered to a halt, and the paranoia freaks drifted back to civilization."

From that, "we" can gather that SEK3 was familiar with the vonuans and their goals, likely from the publications themselves. As can be seen, his perception of them was quite gloomy to say the least.

2) "Carrots And Sticks"

"Before I leave Southern Calif., let me not slight anyone, but simply affirm that there are many libertarians I know well enough to exalt but who have not the general fame for their less persistent endeavors (generally due to working for a living, an affliction found rarely on the E. Coast). And there are others of fame that do not enjoy my personal knowledge, such as Joe Galambos, Natallee Hall and Skye D'Aureous, El Rayo and Naomi Gatherer, and Lou Rollins, whose good and worthy efforts will someday earn them a more adept chronicler."

So, he's highlighting the achievements of various individuals, two of them being Rayo and Naomi Gatherer (aka Roberta, Dr. Gatherer), his freemate.

Additionally, our conception of Rayo during the 1960s and 70s is that he was not very well-known—it seems like he was part of an extremely niche crowd, and, if he enjoyed fame, it was not by the popular definition. That being said, the way Konkin phrases that last portion is interesting: is it possible that Rayo was more popular than "we" originally assumed? Were (or are) there more vonuans than "we" initially figured? Possibly.

3) "Libertarian Strategy (1)"

"So that we are not condemned to relive it, let's review our history. As of December 1968, libertarian strategy was directed either toward influence of the conservatives or conversion of the independents. It was wholly educational or retreatist. Robert LeFevre's Rampart College, Leonard Read's FEE, Joe Galambos' FEI, Nathaniel Branden's NBI, F. A. Harper's IHS, and Frank

Chodorov's ISI were all educational institutes. The VonuLifers, Atlantis group, and Oliverites were seeking escape. Except for the LIBERAL INNOVATOR's leafletting of the Cow Palace in 1964, no libertarians were involved in a political campaign except as deviationist individuals. Many supported Nixon in 1968, but they were clearly of conservative leanings."

...

"Many libertarians also turned inward with incessant psychology sessions and in-group self-criticism. This was the Movement as reflected in 1972 in, say, NEW LIBERTARIAN NOTES, and which could be pieced together from RAP, LIBERTARIAN FORUM, REASON, ACADEMIC ASSOCIATES LETTER, VONULIFE, FREEMAN, SIL NEWS, PACIFIC LIBERTARIAN, and many local newsletters."

Regarding the first quote, SEK3 is quite accurate in stating that VonuLifers were seeking escape. Although Rayo does discuss vonu in cities, he notes that, "I know of quite a few vonuists and libertarians who live [Allen] Humble's way, but I know none who seem to like it for very long." This is mainly due to the city psychological pressures of the statist-servile society, which is why Rayo prefers "to live far enough back in the woods." Other than that minor point, SEK3 is correct.

The second excerpt is particularly interesting, though. Unfortunately, the only VONULIFE articles I have read are those found within Rayo's book and any that have arrived in the batches of vonu publications we've digitized. From that, I certainly don't gather the "incessant psychology sessions" or "in-group self-criticism." Rather, from the entirety of the book, it mainly consists of back-and-forth discussions on strategy, with some philosophy sprinkled in. I'm not sure what SEK3 was referring to here, but it's definitely possible that he's correct—until we acquire a more complete library of those publications, we'll just have to take his word for it.

4) "CounterCampaign '76"

"And who could we all agree on without sacrificing our principles? Behind whom could students of Murray Rothbard, Robert

LeFevre, Ayn Rand, Leonard Read, Joseph Galambos, Karl Hess, Robert A. Heinlein, El Rayo, Natallee Hall, and Harry Browne unite? Nobody."

The point is this: Samuel Edward Konkin III (SEK3) was certainly aware of Rayo and had followed his work. Therefore, we can safely assume, with a lot of evidence and similarities, that agorism is a re-formulation and development upon Rayo's concept of ethical enclaves.

Those aren't all the notable mentions of Rayo or vonu, but we're damn near the end.

In the August 1987 edition of *Liberty Magazine*, two articles discussing Rayo/vonu were published; one by Benjamin Best titled, Tom Marshall: Innovator – A Week in The Wilderness, and the second by R.W. Bradford titled, *The Mystery Man of the Libertarian Movement.*

The full articles can be found at www.vonupodcast.com, so I will only briefly summarize them (just click on Articles About Vonu, below the Start Here tab).

In the first, Best discusses the time he met Rayo in 1967; it was as part of a program Rayo offered called "Vonu Week," wherein individuals visited him in the Siskiyou Region (Northern California/Southern Oregon) to learn about living the wilderness vonu lifestyle. It is definitely valuable, yet this article was published 20 years after-the-fact and Best was awfully fixated on a woman. It's likely not a 100% accurate recollection of his experiences.

The second is more so a Retrospective, wherein Bradford discusses the focus of the libertarian community at the time of Rayo, in addition to how far outside-the-box vonuans were thinking and doing. In regards to Rayo's disappearance, Bradford writes:

"Some people speculate that he grew weary of his paranoid lifestyle and returned to straight society to live an "ordinary life"...But others—those who knew him most intimately—believe he succeeded in achieving vonu, that he continues to live today, deep in the mountains of Southern Oregon, living a fulfilling life as a hunter-gatherer, free at last of the oppression of the state."

Knowing Rayo as intimately as I feel I do, there's no way in hell he could have just given up and returned to the servile society. So, my speculation is that he continued living the wilderness vonu lifestyle, probably mostly in underground structures, until his death.

As far as scouring the Internet, those are all of the honorable mentions I've found of Rayo and/or vonu. It's worth noting that in Jim Stumm's publications (i.e. Self-Liberation Notes, Ocean Freedom Notes, Going Mobile), there are many letters discussing Rayo and/or vonu, but those all took place from the 1970s-1990s. You can download all of them for free by visiting vonupodcast.com.

In conclusion, he certainly had a drastic impact on the libertarian community, even though the majority of the adherents have never heard his name. His contribution of ethical enclaves laid the framework for one of the most popular and efficacious strategies out there today: agorism. For the most radical libertarians of his day, he provided them with solutions in pursuance of personal freedom, when most of the libertarians around him were only interested in "talking" (man, things don't change much, huh?).

His work laid dormant for some 20+ years, but it's back now, and with a vengeance. You, the reader, are the modern self-liberator.

Chapter 3: The "Why" To Vonu

There are still some more preliminary concepts, ideas, and definitions that need to be covered before getting into the "action" of vonu: political crusading, controlled schizophrenia, collective movementism, import-export, and mean-time to harassment. We'll cover the more philosophical ones first and then move onto the couple that interact directly with the "action" side.

As should be clear by now, Rayo and other vonuans were (and are) actually serious about personal freedom and an invulnerability to coercion, which automatically rules out political crusading, a bullshit strategy for bullshit libertarians. Politics, in fact, makes you more vulnerable to coercion (i.e. you're participating in THEIR privacy-unfriendly system). Rayo had this to say:

"The political crusader who wants to take over or destroy a State, **seriously threatens the rulers** and will bring strong countermeasures. But the libertarian who is satisfied to "co-exist" in protracted conflict with the State is merely an annoyance. The more-astute ruler is aware, as is the libertarian, that most people are sheep and will remain sheep no matter how the libertarian lives. Of course the Statist would still rather squash the libertarian if this were easy. So libertarian tactics must be such as to make counter-counterattacks ineffective and prohibitively costly."

Political crusading is also contradictory, speaking in terms of anarchists (or freedom pioneers more generally) consistently living the principles they espouse. Means determine ends and "function determines form." Using the apparatus of the State to achieve freedom shouldn't be taken as a serious consideration by any logical, rational human being.

Political crusading is but one example of the social phenomenon of collective movementism; in other words, naive individuals getting together in large groups, working towards mostly unreachable goals. Not only are these mass social movements anti-individualistic as the individual tends to get lost in the collective, but the larger the membership of an organization, the further away from the original goals it gets, often to the point of unrecognizability.

Just take a look at the modern "Libertarian" and "anarcho-capitalist" movements/communities to view this in action. Both of them started out with quite spectacular aspirations; at the core of these ideologies, private property, peace, and the non-aggression principle (or, as Rayo called it, the ethical principle of non-coercion) were tantamount, and the goal was to build a free society. Anything outside the scope of those items is personal choice, and therefore it is immoral and unethical to interfere with those activities of private persons.

Anarcho-capitalists took it a step further and said, "Okay, so government is immoral and the 'services' they provide are inefficient to put it mildly. The market could better allocate and manage the use of scarce resources, in a peaceful, spontaneous, mutually beneficial manner." So, they theorized about the notions of private justice and arbitration, private policing, and private defense, but only one of those things has really ever been demonstrated – private security/policing by the non-anarchist Threat Management Center in Detroit, Michigan.

Fast forward to today, and the big "debates" in both of these communities are: 1) whether or not anarchists should support State-enforced borders, 2) whether or not "we" should support Dolan J. Tramp, and 3) if "we" should support Augusto Pinochet-style democide and give "our" political enemies free helicopter rides. Surely, people are individuals and there are still great folks who identify with those ideologies; I'm simply speaking of trends.

So, why does this sort of thing happen? How can people go from relatively decent, peaceful human beings to State-worshipping, contradictory fools? Rayo had a term for this phenomenon: "controlled schizophrenia." He only mentions that term explicitly once. I will add the preceding paragraph for context:

"If satisfaction could be plotted with respect to freedom for a large number of people, I think the graph would have a low peak of relative satisfaction around 5% to 10% freedom, a higher peak around 90% to 95% freedom, and wide depression in between.

The lower maximum is exemplified in contemporary society by many a "successful" Middle Amerikan. He lives "conventionally" but takes advantage of some of the easier, more obvious loopholes. He pays income taxes but hires a tax accountant to maximize deductions. He registers for the draft but goes to college in hope of being made a technician instead of a target. His mental state is one of controlled schizophrenia. He believes most of the statist myths in which he was indoctrinated yet maintains a modicum of skepticism. He goes to church, or at least accepts their standard of morality, but is not "above" having a drink at a nude bar. He is largely rational in his work but keeps his rationality compartmented; he does not — dares not critically examine his life as a whole.

Although self-maintained schizophrenia leads to unhealthy and unhappy complications, on the whole the opportunistic serf may have it better than his more consistent, more gullible, less self-motivated brother who is drafted and becomes a target — and a paraplegic rotting in a VA hospital, [or] struggling along in a low-paying, high-taxed job with a load of installment debts."

Other examples of controlled schizophrenics include: "anarchist" politicians, "libertarians" or "anarchists" for Dolan J. Tramp, anarcho-secessionists, state nullification advocates, and political crusaders (generally speaking). All of these folks failed to exorcise the collectivist spooks from their head and ended up backsliding into servile society games, if they ever gave them up at all.

So, a sort of formula can be put together:

Political Crusading + Controlled Schizophrenia + Collective Movementism = Statist/Servile Society

The statist-servile society is the main enemy of the vonuan, the items on the left side of the equation being elements thereof. So, vonuans pursue radical lifestyle changes to become more invulnerable to the coercion of these controlled schizophrenics at-large.

But, how does one gauge whether or not their current lifestyle makes them more invulnerable to coercion and to what degree? Well, right at the outset, Rayo formulated the idea of mean-time to harassment, which he defined as:

"...the strength of vonu, usually expressed in years. MTH is typically used to gauge the profitable viability of concealing a vonuum (the place or situation of an invulnerability to coercion) relative to one's competency at vonumy (the art of achieving an invulnerability to coercion)."

He includes the following visual aid:

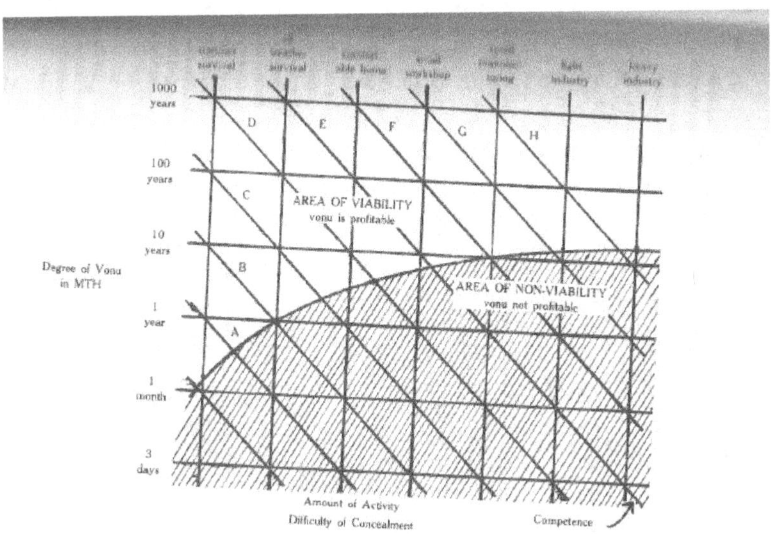

Since the image isn't the clearest, please allow me to explain what's going on here. On the vertical axis, we have the degree of vonu in MTH, or, number of years a vonuan can predict to live undiscovered. On the horizontal axis, we have the difficulty in concealing a vonuum (the place or situation of an invulnerability to coercion), which is equivalent to the amount of activity within said vonu shelters, regardless of what type it is. The chart includes:

- Summer survival
- All weather survival
- Comfortable home
- Small workshop or laboratory
- Small manufacturing
- Light industry
- Heavy industry

So, the idea is that the less mobile/larger a vonuum is, the harder it is to conceal, the higher competency required for the increased activity, and an overall likely drop in the amount of years it will take for it to be discovered.

As a vonuan moves vertically/horizontally in the chart without increasing activity, while also increasing their competence, their MTH will generally increase; if a vonuan moves vertically/horizontally in the chart (increasing activity) without being more competent, their MTH will decrease.

In the chart, there are 8 "levels" of vonu, namely A-H. What vonu lifestyle changes would be applicable for each?

- A, B, and C-level: wilderness vonu, "bugging out"
- D-level: van nomadism
- E-level: off-grid, stationary living (i.e. tiny home living)
- F-level: small manufacturing (i.e. a small workshop)

Here's Rayo's personal take on A-C level vonu:

"The diagonal lines represent levels of capability one order-of-magnitude (10x) apart. Six years ago [in 1967], when I was becoming seriously interested in vonu but had little experience, my competence was roughly represented by line A. Three years ago, after experience with living in a van, competence had increased to line B. Today our competence level is approximated by C. Thus, at present, we can choose among the following: a small tent, adequate for summer only, in a remote place with 100 years MTH; a larger tent and more equipment and supplies in a place with year-round access and a 10 year MTH (the larger tent is also more visible)."

There's one other aspect to point out regarding the above chart: the profitable and unprofitable viabilities. What do Rayo and other vonuans mean by this? Well, in short, the further horizontally one goes on the chart, the more equipment necessary, and the more severe the risk of confiscation becomes. Rayo worded it thusly:

"Within the shaded area vonu is not likely worthwhile – i.e. total costs of being vonu will usually exceed the total benefits. The boundary between the viable and non-viable situations slopes downwards to the left, at least under present conditions. This is because (1) the lower levels of activity require much less equipment and thus a higher probability of confiscation is acceptable; (2) the lower levels of activity are less suspicious and thus unlikely to lead to serious loss even if discovered."

For that reason, G and H-level operations would be huge in scale, making them the least practical, at least for the foreseeable future. Consider Aurora from *Alongside Night*, a sovereign free port, and a new libertarian country as examples of these.

It's worth noting that there may be some inaccuracies in the above explanation. There's only one article wherein Rayo explains MTH and I have to go with what's available, as I can't call him up on Skype and get clarification. Nonetheless, MTH is crucial to vonu, so an honest attempt at fleshing out the idea is at least necessary.

One final element critical to determining one's MTH is Rayo's conception of import-export. He says:

"An optimally-liberated life-style must involve a sort of one-directional isolation. The liberator maintains his access to their open-but-not-free trading centers while denying them access to his home...A freeman obtains information, techniques, key equipment and supplies out of the Servile Society, exporting labor or products in return. And during import-export activities he practices deception – perhaps carries a driver's license ("genuine" or faked); perhaps pays some sales taxes he cannot conveniently avoid. But the freeman's "home base" is physically concealed. There he spends most of his time. There he may sleep, imbibe, love, design, build trade (with fellow freemen), and raise children in relative safety from the savages of State. A freeman's home must be a figurative castle."

At one time, Rayo had hopes that a vonu association or a vonu miniculture would come into fruition, which would eventually develop into an alternative economy. Unfortunately, that still does not exist today (sans deep web marketplaces in a limited context), which necessitates interaction with the statist-servile society, at least to a certain extent. Modern vonuans can only be so self-sufficient; one may have a permaculture farm which produces 100% of the food necessary, a fresh water source allowing him to bypass the need for "city" water, and he may even utilize alternative energy sources allowing him to go "off-grid".

But, what if one of the solar panels breaks and needs to be replaced? I suppose it's possible for him to learn the ins-and-outs of how solar panels work, the components involved, and how to construct it from the ground up, but that doesn't sound like an efficient use of time when he could spend a couple hundred bucks and get one delivered to his house. And, even if this vonuan in question is able to achieve that, what if the tractor he uses for his farm needs a new engine? If his freemate needs a crown on one of her teeth? Maybe his son needs diabetes supplies?

Rayo himself utilized import-export; he purchased bulk, storable foods, replacement glass for the windshield of his van, the polyethylene for his tent, and marijuana for his own personal use (the latter being less important considering his "residence" adjacent to the Emerald Triangle). The point is, there's nothing wrong with utilizing the statist-servile society's "open but not free trading centers," as long as the aforementioned one-directional isolationism is in place.

But import-export isn't only useful for the transacting of goods and products; since said alternative economy is not in place yet, some vonuans choose to or must export their labor to sustain their lifestyles.

Typically, this is done in the form of freelancing, temporary/seasonal employment, trading in ethical enclaves (the black/grey markets of agorism), or basically any other alternative to the servile society's 9-5 grind.

It's worth noting that security culture is of utmost importance when interacting with the servile society. Keep in mind, this society does not respect you as a person; they advocate for violations of your autonomy ad infinitum and many would like to see vonuans tossed in cages by the bludgies for simply holding the philosophical positions they do. Rayo's main recommendation for this was to keep the interaction to a minimum, which he did in one way by getting months of supplies at once, yet there are other strategies you can utilize as well:

- If you're going to be driving to their open-but-not-free trading centers, own an inconspicuous vehicle. For example, a work van draws less attention than an RV if you're living aboard, a Mercury Grand Marquis less than a flashy yellow Corvette, etc. Follow all the traffic laws, have your slave tags up-to-date and visible, keep your automobile clean, and hardest for me, don't blast metal music for all to hear.

- Pay in Federal Reserve Notes (FRNs), digital currencies, or barter; using a credit or debit card makes your movements traceable, and, if the coercers can find you, they can coerce you. If at all possible, try to find like-minded individuals to trade with; support anarchists, libertarians, and/or vonuans, not controlled schizophrenics.

- Role-play police interrogations ahead of time, in case the bludgies try to harass you. When you're pulled over on the side of the road, it's not time for a philosophy lesson, it's not time to tell the bludgie how evil the institution he works for is, nor is it even time for you to plead your case. You've been put in a coercive, potentially violent situation – just try to survive the encounter and deal with any "fallout" after-the-fact.

- Utilize the grey man strategy and blend in with your surroundings. Wear basic clothes, don't open carry an "assault rifle," have situational awareness, and don't initiate conflicts with others.

I'm sure there are others, but that at least gives you an idea.

At some point in the future, as Second Realms and vonu minicultures are created, hopefully the need for import-export will be eliminated; but, for the time being, if vonuans prefer to avoid subsistence living, some interaction with the servile society is necessary.

All of the philosophy and important concepts out of the way, let's begin talking about strategies and lifestyle changes that can make you more invulnerable to coercion. In other words:

> "Now that a collective-movementism (also called bullshit libertarianism and political crusading) has been discredited as a liberation strategy, it is appropriate to re-examine strategies which treat freedom as an individually-achievable way-of-life and marketable commodity."

Section II: The Practice of Vonu

"Whether one will be happier as a freeman or as a slave partly depends
on the individual. But this choice is not open to most libertarians.
Relative contentment in servitude is possible only for those who
believe in it; most libertarians are too independent and well-informed.
For libertarians the choice is between freedom and neurosis." –Rayo,
November 17, 1970, *Libertarian Connection*

Chapter 4: Setting The Stage for Solutions

So, what counts as a vonu freedom strategy? Basically, any lifestyle change that makes the practitioner more invulnerable to coercion. Rayo offered a number of suggestions but it's important to keep in mind that vonu is yours for the making and that:

"A life-style which was vonu 100 years ago may not be vonu today; some life-styles vonu today were not possible 100 years ago and may not be vonu 50 years from now."

In other words, there are no silver bullet solutions and vonu is implemented on an individual basis – what works for me may not work for you and vice versa. It's also important to note that some strategies may not have even been conceived of yet and others may be impossible at present due to technological capabilities (i.e. spacesteading).

Let's begin our examination of potential lifestyle changes in pursuance of personal freedom.

Chapter 5: Go "Gypsy" – NOW!

Nomadic lifestyles seem to be the most efficacious paths towards personal freedom and an invulnerability to coercion. If the coercers can find you, they can coerce you. Constantly moving around can serve as one solution to this problem. There are a number of these nomadic lifestyles, each with its own specific obstacles, initial level of investment capital, and other natural "barriers to entry."

For the freedom pioneer interested in adventure and traveling, nomadic lifestyles may be the answer.

In this section we will cover van nomadism (or, "vehicle nomadism" more generally), minimalist sailboating, perpetual traveling, wilderness vonu, and mobile intentional communities.

Chapter 6: Van Nomadism

Van nomadism was the first strategy Rayo pursued and for good reason — not only is it the easiest lifestyle change in pursuance of freedom, but it just so happens to be the cheapest. As evidence of the latter, ask your average individual in the servile society what their biggest expense is — the answer will almost undoubtedly be housing, regardless of whether they rent or "own."

So, if an individual has decided that the #vanlife is the lifestyle for them, how do they get started? There are two paths that come to mind now: "Just do it" and put together a plan. We'll cover the former first.

Let's say that John has been working in the servile society for 20 years and has $100,000 saved up. He may learn about the lifestyle and pull the trigger immediately, as he has already achieved some level of financial independence. So, he buys a vehicle, whether it's a van, camper, RV, car, or whatever, converts it into a liveaboard rig (if necessary), and moves in as soon as possible.

More power to John, but this is not the most recommended path. Clearly, van nomadism is a radical lifestyle change compared to stationary dwelling; he will likely have some issues adapting early on, especially in trying to figure out what to do with that extra 40+ hours a week not spent in his servile society 9-5 job. The likely drastic shift towards being extremely self-sufficient will probably be difficult as well. Also consider the fact that his vehicle won't be connected to the grid — he will have to learn how to keep up on his hygiene without running water, he'll probably have to get electricity to his rig to power his devices, in addition to just adapting to living in a space the size of an average bathroom, among other things.

One remedy to these problems is to make a plan and take small steps towards the eventual goal of van nomadism.

Take my situation for example. Being a poor 26-year-old, I don't have a nest egg to sustain myself for a year or two on the road, let alone the capital investment necessary to purchase and convert a van at this time. Even worse, I have debt to take care of before I "set sail for sunnier waters." So, for me, this will be a 1-2 year journey, which I'm becoming more and more okay with, as the more time I take, the more prepared I will be. As Jason Boothe, my co-host on **The Vonu Podcast**, always says, "Proper preparation prevents piss poor performance."

Let's take a look at my situation more specifically to see how such a lifestyle could be decided upon and planned for.

I first heard of van nomadism back in mid-2016, when I initially came across Rayo's book. It was interesting, sure, but I had no desire whatsoever to pursue the strategy. Reason being, I was extremely passionate about the prospects of finding freedom on the open ocean (minimalist sailboating, below). But, unfortunately, I didn't have the investment capital to purchase a sailing vessel, I've never sailed a boat, and I still, to this day, have no idea how to traverse the high seas.

So, I continued my research into freedom strategies for another two years, still almost entirely unsure as to what my future would hold...until one weekend on YouTube.

Towards the beginning of 2018, I stumbled across yet another van conversion video and ended up spending the entirety of the weekend (and most of the month) watching similar content. I fell in love with the lifestyle concept and made the decision: "I'm going to be a vonuan van nomad."

It was time to make plans and bring this freer future into reality.

I started by brushing the figurative dust off the Excel spreadsheet containing my frugality budget I had put together a year prior, but failed to stick to for any significant period of time. I updated my income, adjusted my expenses, and re-calculated the amount of money I would have left over. Unfortunately, as I mentioned above, the left over money was not going to savings or my new home on wheels, but was actually going to First Realm banksters in the form of credit card debt (and, at the time of publication, still is).

However, there was (and is) still plenty to do in the meantime. Namely, make frugality a habit, get rid of a bunch of stuff I had no need for (minimalism), adjust my diet to what I envision it being on the road (i.e. little fast food, no microwaveable meals, less meat as it is an expensive source of protein, etc.), conduct market research on vans and take some for test drives to figure out what feels best to me, ponder/plan the van conversion itself (see below), research the best, most affordable, easiest-to-configure off-grid energy setup, build up my freelancing portfolio, generate a handful of passive income streams (this book being one of them), and probably even a few other things, but you get the point.

Even if you aren't ready to live your chosen vonu lifestyle now, there are always things you can do to prepare for it. The above list are all things I'm currently doing, as I'm still paying off the aforementioned debt – although, I'm SO CLOSE. Once that account is closed, the fun truly begins.

Let's talk about those next steps and considerations: purchasing a vehicle for living aboard, the conversion itself, making money on the road, potential legal interstices to exploit, and the modern van nomad community.

Choosing A Vehicle for Living Aboard

This is a crucially important step, but that goes without saying: not only are you purchasing a vehicle, but **you're purchasing your mobile home on wheels**. The vehicle you choose could very well make or break this lifestyle. It could take you on the most incredible adventures and provide you with a significant increase in freedom, or it could lead you down a road of misery.

Recall the saying, "Proper preparation prevents piss poor performance." What sort of considerations should be taken into account?

First and foremost, **space**. How much room do you need to live relatively comfortably with most (if not all) of your belongings? If you'll be vonuing with others, how much more additional space will be necessary? In other words, would upgrading from a Chevy Astro to a Mercedes-Benz Sprinter van (a super common choice) be enough, or are you now in the realm of campers, RVs, or "schoolies"?

Regardless, you're going to have to get rid of some stuff – frugality and minimalism are requirements for **most** van nomads.

Secondly, **your purpose**. What is your purpose for pursuing this lifestyle? Are you going to be a van nomad living in a large city with various squat spots? Are you looking for the most isolated, beautiful, wilderness locations? Maybe a blend of both?

Regardless, this is extremely important. If you're pursuing the former, you'll constantly get harassed with a massive Class A RV; they'll run you out of town one way or another, whether it's the bludgies or the hostile nature of the servile society to alternative lifestyles. Instead, you should find a vehicle that is suited for stealth camping, whether that is a work van or box truck. On the other hand, if you're looking for wilderness adventures, your vehicle will need to be outfitted differently, although, it would still be wise to configure it in such a way that you can stealth camp if necessary.

Thirdly, your **budget**. Do you have a large amount of investment capital, or are you like me and looking for something on the lower end, price-wise?

There are benefits and drawbacks to both, just as with anything in life. If you can afford a new (or newer) Sprinter van, you might be better off by not having to worry about breakdowns or repairs for some time, and you may have a more luxurious home on wheels; but, you'll also have to pay for full coverage automobile insurance on a $30,000+ vehicle. Repairs will likely be more expensive, as well – one vlogging couple I follow spent $15,000 replacing the engine in their Sprinter (granted, they were in Mexico).

Additionally, newer vans come chockful of electronics and those can fail. If they do, you'll likely not be able to fix it, and, even if you are able to, you probably won't have the tools/instruments necessary to do so (they're typically expensive, specialty parts), making you more reliant upon the servile society. If you're traveling through the barren desert, far away from civilization, and a sensor malfunctions on an otherwise perfectly functioning vehicle, you might be dead on the side of the road until help arrives. The more "features," the more that can fail.

It's worth noting the computers and possible Internet connectivity in newer vehicles. These can certainly be used to track your location, making you more vulnerable to coercion, not to mention that these computers can be hacked remotely to take over your vehicle. Recall the bizarre death (murder?) of journalist, Michael Hastings, a few years back, in addition to, I think, the Vault 7 leaks in late 2017. Granted, I highly doubt any vonuan would make themselves such a target where that could actually be possible; if it were, they probably wouldn't be a vonuan, huh?

With older vans, there are less electronics, making them easier to repair yourself. Parts are EVERYWHERE for these vehicles, too — sure, breakdowns can still be expensive and painful, but you'll probably be in a better financial position when it's all said and done. The most common vans that fall into this category are Chevy Express work vans, Dodge Conversion vans, and Ford E-Series vans.

Fourthly, **fuel**. Diesel engines typically get more miles per gallon when compared to unleaded engines of the same size, but they can be more difficult for the average individual to work on, depending upon the vehicle in question. Do some market research of your own and discover what will work best for your situation and applicable expertise.

Lastly, **2-wheel drive or 4-wheel drive**? In my search for vans so far, this has not been a major focus. Reason being, a 2-wheel drive van could get me mostly anywhere I'd want to go, and if I were to ever get stuck on a beach or something, I would have the tools on-hand to get myself out (oh, the things you learn from van nomads on YouTube). That, and from what I know, 4x4 vehicles are more expensive. At this juncture, it's not a necessity or preference for me, but it might be for you. Fantastic! Enjoy those paths further off the beaten trail.

It's also worth mentioning two other possible vehicle choices: a standard car or minivan. Believe it or not, there are quite a few van nomads living out of these super small spaces; some out of necessity, some by choice. If you don't need much, maybe you just decide to hit the road in your Ford F150 with a topper (like one of my Patreon patrons does!). Or, maybe you toss a mattress in the back of your Honda Odyssey, and see where the road takes you.

To close out this section, let's get into a little philosophy. Most everyone has heard of the quote by Benjamin Franklin regarding trading liberty for security.

Similarly, there is a tradeoff between freedom and comfort. Stationary dwellings are quite comfortable. You have air conditioning in the summer, heat in the winter, hot showers twice a day, a flushing toilet, and all of the electricity you could ever use and more, but you are inherently not free, as all of the comforts you enjoy are provided by someone else.

Rayo and Roberta were a living example of this tradeoff, only their choice was on the other end of the spectrum. Wilderness vonuing in the Siskiyou was quite miserable at times and they said as much; but, they were free, both in the physical sense and also according to their mean time to harassment. Clearly, most individuals would not be interested in wilderness vonu, me included. So, the idea is to strike a balance between freedom and comfort; and, thanks to technological advancements, that is quite easy to do nowadays.

As an example, in my van, I'll have a sink powered by a pump, enough solar power to run all of my devices, Internet access via a mobile hotspot (and free Wi-Fi when available), and some sort of a shower system (probably a solar shower). Sure, they may not be as convenient as in my stationary dwelling, but I choose to sacrifice those comforts in pursuance of freedom.

All of that said, this freedom vs. comfort dichotomy certainly comes into play when choosing your vehicle for living aboard. A 2 or 4-wheel drive van can go A LOT more places than a long, slow, and clumsy Class A RV. Choosing one of these larger vehicles will limit your freedom of access to many of the most beautiful, isolated places. But, maybe that's okay for you.

A few final considerations to leave you with:

- If you're going to be buying an older van, MAKE SURE to check the undercarriage for rust.
- Look out for water leaks, as they can lead to mold. The holes can be fixed and mold removed, but it can be a major pain.
- If you're buying a used vehicle, it might be wise to take it to a trusted mechanic before purchasing.
- If you're planning on gutting the back of the van for the conversion, don't pay too much attention to stains on the carpet, torn upholstery, etc.
- These vans, campers, and RVs are everywhere; for the latter two, the best time to buy (I think) is in the winter, after "people return from their summertime escapist rituals and put themselves away in their boxes for another year."

Now you're ready to purchase your mobile home on wheels!

The Conversion

You've purchased your mobile home on wheels – congratulations! What's next? Well, converting it to a live aboard rig. This is the part in the process where you will plan, design, and build out your new abode. It's also the part I'm most looking forward to, in all honesty. If you decide to go the RV or camper route, this might not be as relevant to you, but there will likely still be some modifications since you will be living aboard full-time (or close to it), rather than just using it for weekend getaways. Therefore, the following information should still be valuable.

This is the part where YouTube will be your best friend. Reason being, many van nomads upload videos chronicling every single step of the conversion. I'd also point you in the direction of the old vonu publication, Going Mobile (see "Additional Resources" below); most of this zine is dedicated to letters from van nomads back in the 1960s-80s discussing their rig, living situation, obstacles, etc., but there are also diagrams, pictures, and tutorials on the conversion itself.

For most, the conversion process consists of:

- Gutting the future living space;
- Performing a deep clean of the entire vehicle;
- Patching any holes or leaks, getting rid of any rust, dealing with any mold, etc.;
- Running the wires for the electricity;
- Installing the roof fans/vents;
- Insulating the van (both the floor and the walls, sometimes the roof);
- Laying down the flooring and putting up the walls;
- The rest of the build out (i.e. whatever you decide upon).

Obviously, this process may vary depending upon the individual and the situation, but these are the main steps.

Important Notes: Make sure to run the wires for the electricity BEFORE installing the insulation and the walls. Also, don't half-ass your electrical setup; do it right the first time. Pay an experienced electrician to help you, if need be. It's cheaper and less painful than your mobile home going up in flames from some silly, avoidable mistake.

What are some other considerations to take into account?

What are **your needs**? This is the most important question and will determine the complexity or simplicity of the process. If you've never lived out of a vehicle before, you probably won't know the full answer to this question. Therefore, it is recommended that you take practice runs before moving aboard. This way, you can determine whether or not this lifestyle is for you, in addition to discovering what you really, truly need.

Some individuals go with barebones conversions. For example, John may decide to toss a mattress in the back of his minivan, grab some gallon jugs of water, some food, and a camp stove and hit the road.

Others, like Karl and Jahla, a vonuan van nomad couple traveling Australia, go all out with the conversion. You can view images of their exquisite rig below, but I would recommend checking out the van tour – their website is www.comfortablylost.com. You can find links to all of their social media accounts there.

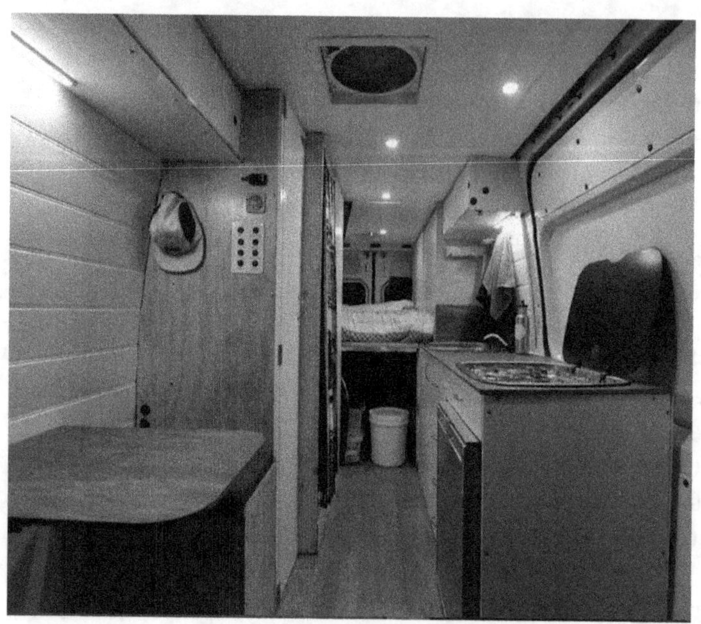

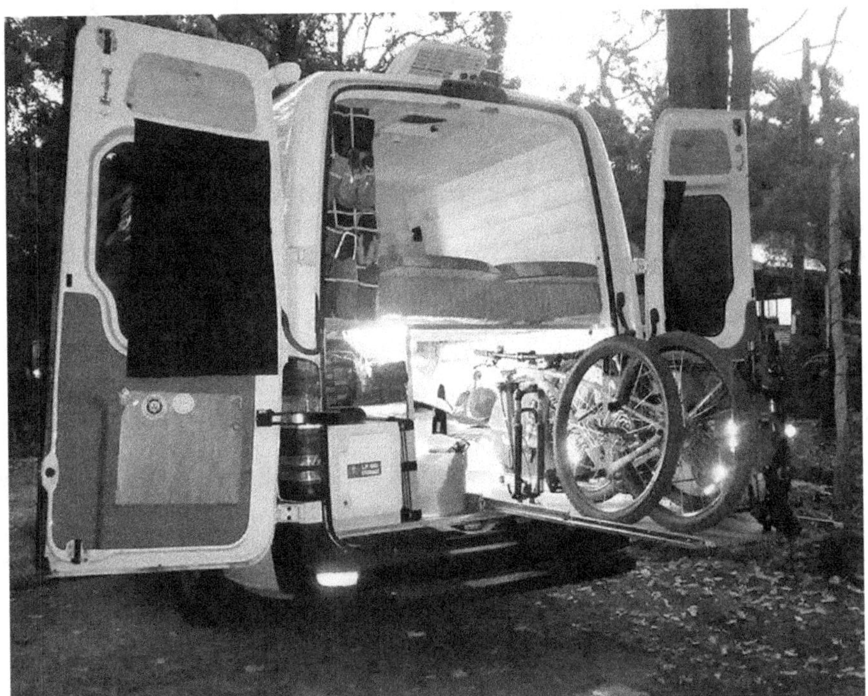

As you can see, Karl and Jahla spent quite a bit of money on their van and the subsequent conversion – easily more than $50,000 in total (an expensive car but a cheap home). But, you don't have to spend that much; hell you can spend as much or as little as you want.

I've seen conversions ranging from $500 all the way up to $20,000. Most van nomads will fall somewhere in the middle, but that doesn't mean you can't have a beautiful, functional, and comfortable mobile home. Here are some features you'll undoubtedly add during your conversion:

- A bed
- A kitchen area (possibly a cooking stove and a sink; be sure to vent this outside to avoid carbon monoxide poisoning)
- Storage – lots and lots of easily accessible storage space
- A way to dispose of human waste
- Some sort of a system to keep up on hygiene (i.e. a shower, wet wipes to hold you over until your next visit to Planet Fitness, etc.)
- Roof vent

- Electricity source (gas generator, solar power, wind power, etc.)
- Blackout curtains for privacy if you have windows
- Locks inside and out for safety and privacy

Here are some other important considerations to take into account:

- Make sure EVERYTHING is secured in the vehicle, the big, heavy things most importantly. You don't want your belongings launching across your vehicle in transit; and, God forbid, if you were to get in a high-speed accident, you don't want those to turn into projectiles.
- Use lightweight materials when converting your vehicle and keep track of all of the weight you'll be adding to it. Try your best to keep it under the maximum recommended weight; reason being, overloading your vehicle will impact the handling, braking, gas mileage, etc.

Don't let the perfect be the enemy of the good, though. Keep in mind, pursuing vonu is a lifelong endeavor. As you gain more experience and become more competent, you will always find ways to improve upon your vonu home base. Hence, why many YouTube van nomads have multiple conversion series on their channel.

I could go into a lot more depth, but considering the communication format of this medium, I'll stop here and turn you over to the modern van nomad community on YouTube. They're seriously a helpful bunch.

Making Money on The Road

Most individuals pursuing van nomadism will be leaving their full-time job in the servile society; some will have savings enough to live for many years and others will have to find ways to make money on the road.

Looking at damn near 100 different case studies (i.e. van nomads), the average cost-per-month for this lifestyle is $500-$1,000 a month, or $6,000-$12,000 a year. This includes the following, core expenses:

- Car Insurance
- Food

- Gas
- Planet Fitness Membership
- AAA Membership
- Cell Phone Plan (mobile hotspot optional)
- Basic Health Insurance
- Vehicle Repair and Maintenance

There will likely be additional expenses, but those will be determined on an individual basis. For example, I need to factor in diabetes supplies (test strips, insulin), vape juice for my vape pen, and medical cannabis, as I will first be venturing out to Colorado in an attempt to cure or at least treat this dreaded autoimmune disease.

Some may fear the unknown: "How will I make enough money to survive on the road?" Now that you know the average cost of this lifestyle, I hope that fear has been quelled, at least to a certain extent. It's not difficult to make $1,000/month (the higher end) if you are willing to work.

So, what are some ways to generate that income?

First off, as I mentioned above, many vonuans utilize temporary and seasonal employment. When I venture to Colorado, I plan on taking temporary jobs at ski resorts (free lift passes!), but it's not limited to that, of course. This is a terrific option for vonuans. Please allow me to explain below.

- Situation: An individual takes a three-month seasonal position at the going rate of $10/hour. He nets $400/week, $1,600/month, and $4,800 for the entire gig (the theft known as taxation not included).
- If he/she is living on $750/month, that comes to $2,250 in living expenses during the time of the temporary position.
- That leaves the individual in question with $2,550 in savings, or 3 months of the van nomad lifestyle when it's all said and done.

So, hypothetically, a van nomad could take two, three-month long seasonal jobs a year and live comfortably, while having the other half of the year open for adventure. That sounds like a sweet life, right? It puts the "2 weeks of vacation," servile society "benefit" to shame.

But, there are other avenues available to van nomads, like creating self-liberational media. Believe it or not, van nomadism is kind of trending. You could leverage that to make some additional income by starting a YouTube channel, a website/blog, you could write a book and sell it, etc.

One cautionary note: YouTube has been known to shut down and de-monetize channels for no reason at all. Get while the gettin's good, as the saying goes, but do not rely upon it. The smart vonuan will never rely upon one single source of income, anyways.

Digital nomadism more generally is probably the most popular way van nomads make money on the road. This typically consists of freelancing or an entrepreneurial business of some sort. Do you have any marketable skills you could leverage? Think graphic design, website design, coding and development, online marketing, or a consulting biz. These are in-demand and businesses/corporations often hire freelancers at higher rates, as it is a lot cheaper than hiring a formal employee.

There are three other potential options I learned about from other van nomads. Apparently, individuals have had some success with posting "gigs wanted" ads on Craigslist and Facebook (option 1 and 2). If you're rolling into a town and need to make some quick cash, you might try that. I've heard the money isn't always great and that it can sometimes turn into some tedious odd jobs, but regardless, it's an option if you're in a crunch.

The third option is actually quite incredible for van nomads: delivery/driving services like Uber, UberEats, Postmates, etc. If you're ever in a crunch and need to make some money, find a larger city and do some delivering. As long as you have a smartphone, you're almost always in a position to make money. That's huge.

Quitting your job in the servile society can surely be daunting; it can put your life in question and cause a lot of stress – but it doesn't need to. The van nomad life is quite cheap and there are seemingly endless ways to make money on the road. The only limitations are your creativity and imagination.

Jurisdictional Arbitrage, Legal Interstices, and Tricks for Van Nomads

Jurisdictional arbitrage is defined as the practice of taking advantage of discrepancies between competing legal jurisdictions. This is generally practiced between countries and nation-states, but it can be applied here in so-called "America" as well. Similarly, legal interstices are defined as grey areas within the law that can be used to violate the spirit of the law while simultaneously keeping the letter of the law.

Take my last place of residency: The Communist State of Illinois. This hellhole is most well-known for being home to the former crime capital in the world, crippling business regulations, a higher price to pay for anything you want to do, and a mass exodus of citizens into other legal jurisdictions.

So, what sort of jurisdictional arbitrage methods and interstices are available to me and other van nomads? A legal mailing address, vehicle registration, and residency.

The state of South Dakota must seriously be hurting for revenue. In most states, the process for these things is difficult, expensive, time consuming, and there are always hurdles to jump through. Thankfully, South Dakota wants your money so bad, they will jump through the hurdles for you making it easy to become (or remain) "legally compliant".

The first item to discuss is the legal mailing address, as this is a requirement for all of the others. One of the logistical issues with a nomadic lifestyle is mail forwarding. You might not always know where you're going to be, how long you're going to be there, and if what is being delivered can be earmarked for general delivery.

Enter, YourBestAddress.com.

For $189/year, you can setup custom shipping schedules. For example, if you're going to be in Denver, Colorado for a few weeks working a short-term gig, you simply put in a request to have your mail forwarded there. There are other features, such as: $1 handling fee per shipment (lowest out there), free junk mail sorting, email notification for outgoing mail, no hidden postage fees, and even a couple other, more minor ones. Better yet, this isn't a mere post office box. This is a LEGAL, physical mailing address, and the first step for the other interstices this website offers.

Next is vehicle registration. Here in Illinois, it costs $128 for me to register my 1998 Mercury Grand Marquis yearly. In South Dakota, its $45, and you can mail-in the necessary forms using the address you signed up with before. You don't even have to physically go to the state. Here's the process:

- Application for Motor Vehicle and Registration

- An original Title or Manufacturer's Statement of Origin (if new) properly transferred to the applicant
- A Bill of Sale, sales contract, or purchase order
- Vehicle weight (empty)
- A copy of your current driver's license
- The current odometer reading

Obviously, the bureaucratic bullshit sucks, but it's something you'll have to deal with regardless.

That's not all though. Here in Illinois, the excise tax on a new or used vehicle is 6.25%; in South Dakota, it's 4% with no vehicle inspections or emissions tests. Let's say you decide to buy a brand new Chevy Express work van which comes out to $30,000. In Illinois, the excise tax would be $1,875. In South Dakota, it would be $1,200. So, utilizing YourBestAddress.com could net you a savings of $758 in the above example. It may not seem like a whole lot, but why wouldn't you do it if the process was the same, easier even?

Next is residency. Now obviously, as vonuans, the goal would be to avoid becoming a citizen of any government, but unfortunately, that's not very practical. Therefore, since most everyone will choose residency in some state, why not choose the one with the most legal benefits? Become a South Dakota resident in under 24 hours!

Once you've obtained your physical address, you simply complete the required government forms (gross!), stay one night in a hotel, RV park, or AirBnB, and trudge on down to a South Dakota Department of Motor Vehicles office. The local bureaucrat will ask you for the receipt from where you stayed, you'll provide one document proving your identity, date of birth, and lawful status, one document verifying your Social Security Number, and you're done. You're now a resident of South Dakota and it took less than a day!

And you aren't even required to live in South Dakota; hell, you don't even have to visit again if you don't want to.

So, what makes South Dakota advantageous in terms of legal interstices? They put together this list:

- Becoming a resident is simple and painless
- You will pay no state income tax, as there is none
- No inheritance tax

- No personal property tax
- No annual vehicle inspections
- Low cost registration fees
- 4% sales tax

Compared to The Communist State of Illinois, those benefits could certainly be beneficial.

Now that all of the governmental nonsense is out of the way, I'd like to conclude this section discussing three tips and tricks that might help you in pursuit of this lifestyle.

First is hygiene – how do van nomads stay clean? Well, some van nomads have showers aboard their rigs; others are in the wilderness enough that taking a dip in the creek suffices; but, almost all van nomads have a membership to Planet Fitness. It really is a no-brainer.

For $21/month, you have access to their shower and workout facilities – and Planet Fitness's are EVERYWHERE. The regular, hot showers are great, sure, but what if it rains for a few days straight and you are cooped up in your van? Cabin fever is not outside the realm of possibilities. Being able to get out of your van to workout would seemingly be a major blessing.

But, that's not all. With your Planet Fitness membership, you'll also have access to unlimited use of hydromassage, unlimited use of massage chairs, free haircuts, and free WiFi, among other things! So, you could do your morning #vanlife vlog, go workout and shower, upload your video to YouTube, and get a haircut.

So, I'd recommend you pony up that $21/month. You'll be glad you did.

Next is a AAA membership. If you aren't familiar, this yearly subscription service offers roadside assistance, emergency battery service, fuel delivery, lock-out services, tire services and more. They offer three different tiers: Classic ($58/year), Plus ($93/year), and Premier ($123/year).

As an example, let's take a look at their mid-level tier. For your subscription, you qualify for:

- Up to four 100 mile tows
- Emergency starting
- Battery service

- Flat tire service
- Fuel delivery
- Vehicle locksmith service
- Extrication/winching
- Car travel interruption
- Emergency check cashing

And more. Breakdowns happen; they're inevitable. Don't leave yourself stranded, forced to pay for a tow that will inevitably cost more than a yearly AAA membership.

Lastly, is medical. Clearly, without a full-time, 9-5 job, it's safe to say that most van nomads go without health insurance. So, how do van nomads get dental work done, medical care, or medical supplies? This was one of the major hurdles for me: without healthcare, there is no way in hell I could afford my diabetes supplies, mostly thanks to the fascistic, socialistic healthcare system here in so-called "America."

So, how did I overcome this obstacle? I posted in a couple van nomad groups on Facistbook, and lo and behold, there are other diabetic van nomads! Within minutes, the biggest hurdle was out of the way, and the answer is Algodones, Mexico.

Algodones is smack dab on the border of Mexico and Arizona, a short 25 minute drive from Yuma, Arizona. Algodones has been featured in such publications as Forbes Magazine for their high quality medical tourism industry. Many van nomads have documented their trips there and it basically looks like an American city, albeit without the ridiculous barriers to entry. English is the primary language so you won't have problems communicating with your dentist, pharmacist, or doctor.

So, what about the cost? Believe it or not, you can get the same prescriptions and medical care as you would here in America, but for a far cheaper cost, even without health insurance. Ah, the free(r) market!

As another alternative, you **can** obtain healthcare without going through an employer here in the US. For example, I recently found out that I can get basically the same health insurance I had when gainfully employed, for just a little more a month -- $245/month to be exact, versus ~$150 or so. Clearly, I'd rather not have to pony up that monthly payment, but it beats the hell out of paying full-price for diabetes supplies.

I'm sure I'll learn a bunch of other tips and tricks once I hit the road, but these are the most common ones.

So, why should you consider van nomadism as your first vonu lifestyle change?

- It's the easiest lifestyle change available.

Unlike sailing the open ocean, most everyone has experience driving a car. Sure, there are some obstacles and hurdles, but they aren't too much to deal with for the dedicated freedom pioneer.

- It's one of the cheapest lifestyles out there.

Recall the average monthly cost for this lifestyle: $500-$1,000/month. Most people pay that much or more for their stationary dwelling in the servile society. With that expense out of the way, this enables you to work less and utilize that time doing whatever you decide to do.

Also consider that when individuals lose their jobs or their homes, what are they sometimes relegated to doing? Living out of their car. Now, obviously, this scenario isn't by choice, but that alone should really illuminate the fact that this lifestyle is extremely cheap.

- It's immensely freeing and rewarding.

What if you could make all the money you needed (and more) working half of the year and doing whatever you wanted for the rest of it? What if your scenery and "front porch" view could change from the desert one day, to the ocean the next? What if you weren't tied down to a fixed location for years on end, working a job you hate, to pay for a house that you basically (likely) only sleep in? Better yet, what if all of those things were well within reach?

- Van nomadism is a terrific interim lifestyle.

For me, the dream is still to find freedom on the open ocean, but I'm not going to wait around to be free. Therefore, van nomadism serves as a great interim lifestyle. In Vonu, Book 2: Letters from Rayo, he writes:

"I have never maintained that motorized-nomadism is a panacea. I did choose it for and have found it to be an excellent INTERIM life-style for someone still extensively involved in the servile society (through earning money, seeking a woman, etc.)."

Even if your end goal is something different, why not begin to live free in the here and now?

- The modern van nomad community is incredible: you don't have to do this alone.

As I said, van nomadism is kind of trending right now. One YouTube search will garner months of content, but this van nomad community does not only exist in the digital realm; it also exists in the physical realm.

This is one of the things I'm most looking forward to: many of these folks are vonuans, they just have never heard of the word. These are individuals who, for whatever reason, decided that a normal life in the servile society was not for them. Instead of political crusading and begging the masters to change the system, they pursued direct action and created the life they desired themselves. Even if we have differing economic opinions or whatever, these people are serious. And I can't wait to meet them.

To give you an idea of how many van nomads are out there, let me tell you about RTR, or the Rubber Tramp Rendezvous. Every January in Quartzite, Arizona, van nomads from all across North America meet for a week in the desert to mingle, learn from each other, and get help in building out their vans. In 2018, some 4,000 nomads were in attendance. I'm hoping to attend in 2020 – by that time, there will likely be well over 5,000 nomads in attendance.

To conclude, I'll end with a quote from a nomad who wrote into INNOVATOR in March 1968:

"So far I have been too busy to travel extensively or to seek out especially attractive campsites. But already I have lived many exquisite days and evenings at beaches, mountains and forests. I am still learning the way of a modern nomad, **but already I am free.**"

Chapter 7: Wilderness Vonu

Wilderness vonu was Rayo and Roberta's preferred vonu lifestyle after they discovered van nomadism was not freeing enough for them. It is the most radical and one of the most difficult, too. Your average individual in the servile society would likely be dead within a couple weeks if they were airdropped into the middle of the wilderness.

Since most folks would never seriously consider this as a viable option, I'm not going to spend much time on it, and for those that do, Rayo's vonu publications will be far more worthwhile than any attempt I could make to explain it.

Below is an article by Rayo from Vonu Life, March 1973 titled Smumans: The Super Hobos. Herein, you'll discover how such a nomadic, wilderness lifestyle could be achieved, the various vonu home bases involved, how interaction could be facilitated between other smumans, and how various vonu lifestyle changes can be combined, among other things. Enjoy.

SMUMANS: THE SUPER HOBOS
By: Rayo

'Smum' stands for Seclusion and Mobility Using Multiplicity. Smum has some features of and intergrades with troglodyte, foot-nomad, urban anonymity, and vehicle-nomads ways, but is [it] differs in overall living pattern and equipment use. Smum has similarities to traditional ways as diverse as hobos, eskimos, fur trappers with several overnight cabins, and wealthy families with several 'conventional' houses.

Many smum life-styles are possible but all involve migration among various abodes. The abodes are usually simple, inexpensive, semi-permanent and widely separated. A number of towns of a region are used, in succession, as trading outposts. Smum offers, in part the wide-ranging mobility and anonymity of vehicle nomadism with the privacy and safety of troglodysm. While smum is complicated to describe (at least with conventional concepts), smum is easier to implement than any other life-style I presently know of which offers comparable vonu. Smum is made economical by the low cost of plastic film and second-hand utensils.

A smum family migrates between its abodes, probably seasonally. Less often an abode is moved to a new site within the same area, or phased out in favor of a new abode developed elsewhere.

Most of the abodes are located at least a quarter-mile and not more than ten miles from a road. The road is preferably either a highway, or a trail without habitation along it or at its intersection with the highway. Most abodes cannot be reached by motor vehicles. There are several hiking routes from each abode to one or more such roads. Each route reaches the road at a different place and at a place out of sight of residences. At least one route from each abode ends in a parking spot which is out of sight of the road and rarely used – suitable for unloading supplies.

A few hundred yards into the brush from each parking spot is a stash for low-value supplies awaiting backpacking to the abode. The supplies are stored in drums for protection from animals and weather.

Hiking routes are irregular and cannot be followed by someone not familiar with them. Each route is used only a few times a year so it doesn't receive much wear.

In Siskiyou region, abode sites are selected so that highway distance between is typically 100 miles. This separation is determined be the distance between major trade towns and the living patterns of conventional people – people rarely go a hundred miles to work, shop or socialize. Overland hiking distance between abodes is less – typically 30 to 40 miles – the abodes all lying within the same mountain range.

A family has no single trading outpost. From each abode a different town or, better yet, two or three in alternation are used for shopping, receiving forwarded mail, and perhaps temporary employment. The towns so used are fairly large – at least 5,000 people within shopping range. And they are located on major highways and thus accustomed to many visitors.

After living at one abode a few months and making trips alternately to the nearest suitable towns (which preferably lie in opposite directions) the family moves to another abode, a hundred miles away, and makes trips to different towns. And so forth. They do not return to the first abode and the corresponding trading outposts until a year has passed. If a family has six abodes, 12 trading towns, and makes trips to town twice a month, one member is in each town twice a year, not often enough to be distinguishable from the many thousand travelers who stop briefly.

The family is probably not limited to a fixed schedule or route. If they encounter trouble in one town they do not return to that area for several years, meanwhile developing a new abode elsewhere. In an emergency they can hike overland between abodes without using roads or going into populated areas.

All possessions of a smum family have one or more of the following characteristics: inexpensive, expendable, small, used seasonally. Inexpensive items are duplicated and left at each abode. These might include polyethylene film and rope for rigging tents, bedding, cooking stove, utensils, extra clothes, and drums for storage while abode is not occupied. Bedding, clothes and utensils are scavenged at dumps or purchased second hand. Total cost of stationary items at a warm-weather abode is probably less than $50. Expendable supplies include food staples, soap, writing paper, kerosene and propane. These are ordinarily left at an abode until consumed. Some small but valuable items move with the family; such things as watch, transistor radio, binoculars, handgun, radiation detector, camera, medical kit, sewing kit, and often-used reference books. Seasonal items are grouped according to use at specific abodes; these include most books, tools and construction materials.

Each abode is somewhat specialized for the activities performed there and the season that it is used. Abode might include:

Summer camp: This may be more remote than other abodes since there will usually not be snow and swollen rivers to hinder access. If foraging and vonu horticulture are accomplished in that area, books, tools, and preservation equipment are stored there. A plastic tent and mosquito netting are sufficient shelter.

Winter abode: This may be a semi-underground structure, or a large foam hut plus a plastic tent. Since there is little warm working space much reading and writing are done there. Most books are stored there.

Electric abode: A small generator, probably hydroelectric, powers a sewing machine, electronic equipment, or any other gear requiring electricity but not bulky imports. Relevant books and materials are stored there.

'Edge place': This is for work involving bulky imported materials such as carpentry, and is the one abode accessible to vehicles. Major work on any vehicles is performed there; also any work which because of space required, noise or smells is not easily vonued. Edge place is most likely on fairly secluded private land leased from a friendly landowner. An old van or house trailer may be parked there to provide sheltered work and storage space. Edge place is much less vonu than other abodes so work requiring much privacy is not performed there. And any family members especially threatened, such as slave-age children during that season, remain elsewhere.

A minimally-furnished van may be used for shelter if one or more members occasionally go into that society to earn money. When not in use it is probably parked on private land, perhaps at edge place.

A friend who may be outside the Siskiyou region provides a permanent mailing address. The friend accumulates mail, bundles it, and sends it as a parcel, as directed. If possible the family makes arrangements with trustworthy local people in each town to receive U.P. parcels; if not the parcels come general delivery.

A legal home address for drivers license and vehicle registration, if needed, is probably arranged in a large city outside the region, and separate from the mailing address.

Means of transportation vary. One smuman may not have any vehicle. *E* hitchhikes for mail and light supplies, also for migration between abodes. *E* hires a van or pickup, preferably a transient, to haul heavier supplies.

Another smuman may use a motorcycle for all transport – this will be a bike with enough power for the highway yet light enough to manhandle into hiding places – perhaps a 250cc trail bike.

Still another may have a van or camper for hauling supplies as well as for work excursions. *E* will also use a motorbike or else hitch rides, since places suitable for long-time parking will seldom be convenient to unloading spots.

Smumans, like other vonuans, obtain money in ways which minimize time and involvement with the Servile Society. One may have a line of special services or products *e* sells thru merchants in the towns *e* visits. Another may have a mail-order enterprise. Someone with a highly-paid skill may journey to a distant city for temporary employment.

But most, at least at first, will probably depend on day labor in nearby towns and seasonal crop work. Although this is low paying, a smuman's expenses can be very low. So not many day's work are needed.

An individual or family without slave-age children can be flexible about outside employment – working together or separately at any time of the year. A family with children is more constrained. Perhaps during the school year the children remain at a secluded site, then during Summer the whole family does crop work and any other activities involving that society.

If asked for address by employers or bludg, a smuman gives *er* legal home address. If asked for local address *e* says *e* is visited by some friends (location vaguely defined).

A smuman can be opener with outsiders than can be a more-stationary wilderness-vonuan. In some instances *e* may be able to socialize with local non-vonuans. *E* can even say to friends *e* is camping 'back in the woods', knowing *e* will have moved on to other woods before the word gets very far.

For a smuman, the whole Siskiyou region becomes, in a sense, a single widely-dispersed city of several hundred thousand people. Smum offers much of the anonymity of metropolis without the pollution or nuclear danger. Assets are dispersed and cannot be destroyed by a single misfortune.

Comparing smum to full-time van living: Most time is spent in or around abodes which are concealed away from roads in rugged, brushy areas rarely if ever penetrated. With our van the greatest mean time to harassment (mth) we have achieved is one or two years. Whereas with a small tent we can easily achieve 20 years mth; with more work and care, 200 years mth. (Interpretation: if there are 200 such camps, an average of one a year will be discovered.) This is while a camp is set up; torn down and stuffed in drums under bushes chance of discovery is even lower. We have had enough stash tents in enough situations to have confidence in the 20 year figure. One year mth is adequate for someone not especially threatened who wants peace and quiet. It is not sufficient for slave-age children, someone without 'acceptable' ID, or for most kinds of alternate-economy enterprises.

A serious disadvantage of smum for some: activities must be accomplished at certain places and in certain seasons, rather than when one is in the mood. Planning and bookkeeping are essential. Life is more structured than with everything in one place, but the structure is chosen by oneself, not imposed by outsiders.

One might initiate a smum life-style by exploring a region on foot and hitchhiking, using light-weight camping gear, then gradually build equipment and supplies at the most desirable spots. Or a van nomad might develop a string of vehicle squat-spots; then use these as bases for scouting. On the other hand, from a smum life-style one can become, say, a troglodyte by further developing one abode and phasing out the others.

Like any new life-style, smum should be begun when one is not in immediate danger --- when one has time to experiment and can survive a few mistakes.

Chapter 8: Minimalist Sailboating

99.9% of land here on Planet Earth has been laid claim to by some government, which would suggest that there aren't many places self-liberators can go to be free. When it comes to stationary dwellings on land, that is certainly true, especially considering the fee simple system of land ownership here in at least "America," if not in every other nation/country as well. There really is no such thing as private property when it comes to land ownership – the State truly is your landlord. If you don't believe me, try not paying your "yearly rent," otherwise known as property taxes. You'd be lucky to only have the landlord come a knockin'.

Not to mention other issues that may arise with "owning' land, such as nuisance abatement (which is extremely relevant if one is going to be off-grid homesteading), the difficulty of picking up and moving if necessary, and obviously, the expensive cost of stationary dwellings, among other things.

That said, **71%** of this planet is made up of wide open ocean. This translates into over **332,519,000** cubic miles of water, as estimated by the U.S. Geological Survey. And yet, in large part, humans have yet to even begin utilizing the seemingly endless possibilities abound. As Rayo said:

"If your State of anchorage becomes intolerable, don't waste energy in extended public criticism or conflict; apply your free market principles by setting sail for sunnier waters." –Rayo, INNOVATOR, March 1967

Let's begin by discussing the arbitrary boundaries selected and enforced by current nation-states.

- Contiguous Zone: A band of water extending from the outer edge of the territorial sea up to 24 nautical miles (27.6 miles) from the baseline, within which a state can exert limited control for the purpose of preventing or punishing infringement of its customs, fiscal, immigration or sanitary laws and regulation.

- Exclusive Economic Zone: Extends from the outer limit of the territorial sea to a maximum of 200 nautical miles (230.2 miles) from the territorial sea baseline…A coastal nation has control of all economic resources within its exclusive economic zone…However, it cannot prohibit passage or loitering above, on, or under the surface of the sea.

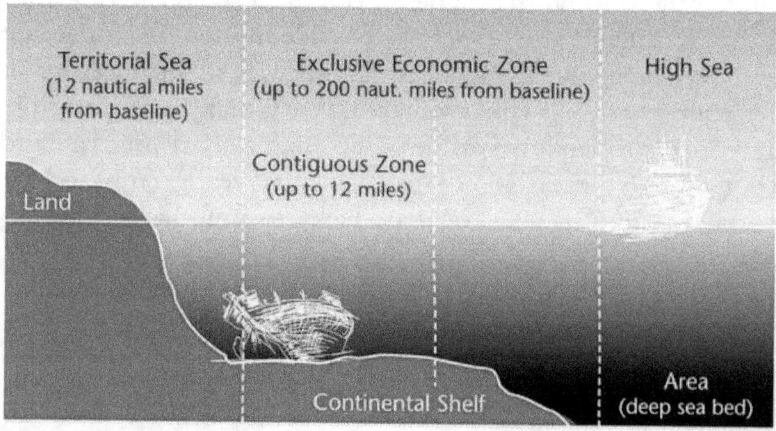

[Note: "Territorial" is on the image above, but that's not helpful for our purposes as vonuans. That is the servile society. Some folks have gotten away with docking their live aboard boats at marinas for years upon years, but local governments tend to be shutting that down now via nuisance abatement.]

Reason would dictate then, that as long as a vonuan is at least 24.1 nautical miles off the coast of an existing nation/country, they are, for the most part, outside of any government's jurisdiction; that is, unless they are mining minerals off the ocean floor, attempting to deliver or manufacture nuclear weapons, or if they are a part of an international drug smuggling ring. As the description said above, a government cannot stop you from crossing their EEZ. Obviously, as vonuans, "we" know not to rely upon these legal interstices, but its necessary information to possess regardless.

All of that said, when would sailing vonuans have to deal with the coercion of the bludgies?

1. When an individual is beginning their journey; namely, when they are obtaining their flag of convenience. In short, international law requires a ship to be registered in a country, or else you'll be regarded as a pirate.

2. When an individual is entering the port of a country; I don't know what this process consists of, but there will be dealings with bludgies. They might search your boat.

Outside of those two scenarios, there shouldn't be any other interactions with government, especially if you are spending most of your time on the high seas.

Case Study: City Jim to Captain Jim

Jim Smith spent his entire childhood and most of his thirties in the communist hell-hole known as New York City. He graduated with an engineering degree from Columbia University only to end up as a contractor for Boeing, putting together the next design for the military's F-35 fighter jets. And he truly did love the work.

"I made it," he thought to himself. "I'm 24 years old and I'm pulling in six-figures."

Fast forward a few years, and he is happily married to his wife, Katie. They actually met each other in a mosh pit at a killer Veil of Maya show. In a normal context, the way they met probably would have been considered spousal abuse, but in this circumstance, it was love at first accidental-elbow-to-Katie's-face.

They are in a great financial situation for their age (statist-servile society standards, that is), but they aren't positive if they want to rear offspring or not. They decide to put it off a few years.

Jim is still plugging away at Boeing. He's received numerous commendations for his superior work, but they just aren't doing much for him anymore; the law of diminishing returns in action, maybe? Not so much. When he was younger, he didn't much care what the product of his labor was used for; he didn't even think about it. He was there to collect his weekly paycheck so he could go chase women at nightclubs and that was it.

Then the Bradley Manning leaks happened. He saw the realities of war firsthand and realized that his job was far more than just schematics and mathematics: he was producing weapons of mass murder. It was then that he knew he HAD to make a change. He requested an internal re-assignment to private sector work but it was denied. So, he quit, unsure as to what his future may hold.

When he went home, he vented his frustrations and outrage to an understanding Katie. Like most, she really didn't have any idea what was going on in the geopolitical realm, but she could see that this was eating Jim up inside, and rightfully so. She decided to retreat to her office to think.

After some thorough research on the Internet that evening, Katie came across a podcast episode titled, "The Antiwar Rayo," released by two folks, Shane and Jason. They laid down in their bed and listened together before they went to sleep. This was the start of their journey as vonuans.

Over the course of the next few weeks, they scoured all of the content currently available on this freedom strategy called "vonu" and this really interesting guy named Rayo. They sold their house, got rid of 98% of their belongings, bought a brand new Mercedez-Benz Sprinter van, converted it into a live aboard rig, and travelled across the US for the next few years.

They enjoyed the van nomad lifestyle but realized it wasn't exactly where they would like to be. They recalled Rayo's quote about "setting sail for sunnier waters" and decided to invest in a 49' Jeanneau Sun Odyssey sailboat. Since neither of them have any experience in this realm, they took some boating classes and paid an experienced skipper to take them out a few times. They took it slow, but they were adept in no time.

After a couple years on the water, they decided they wanted to have a child; they were only getting older and the years were running out. Surprisingly enough, they had twins, Alice and Frank. After ensuring the babies were healthy and spending some time settling in as parents, they set sail as a family for the very first time. When Alice and Frank get a little older, Jim and Katie plan on unschooling them.

Case Study: From Skipping School to Skipper

Nathan Scott (somehow) graduated high school this year and, like most high school-aged kids, he has no idea what he wants to do with his life. He's in a more interesting situation, though, compared to his peers.

When he was a freshman, he came across the Bad Quaker Podcast, hosted by a guy named Ben Stone. Ben introduced Nathan to the concept of anarchism, a label he now proudly proclaims. His parents think he's just trying to be "cool," but he has extremely good philosophical, ethical, economic, and practical reasons for his hatred of the State.

And he's passionate about the idea of freedom. He's a regular listener to The Vonu Podcast and he knows higher level indoctrination (college) is not for him. Hell, he knows a normal, 9-5 servile society job would drive him mad. He's considered van nomadism as an interim lifestyle, but he agrees with Rayo: the strategy's reliance on "slave tags" is unsettling. So where does that leave young Nathan?

He wants to set sail for sunnier waters. He has no idea what he's doing, has no money to do it, but he's made his goal. And, as a dedicated freedom pioneer, he won't take no for an answer. Thankfully, his young age means that he has no debt to take care of, no "affairs" to get in order (i.e. selling a house), and no one dependent upon him. He can safely take some risks, especially considering he's on his parents' health insurance for another 8 years.

Living on the west coast, he knows that there are occasionally positions open at marinas or docks for maintenance, service, and janitorial duties. "At least," he thinks to himself, "this will be a start. I can learn the basics and go from there." So, he applies for an open dock position and gets it.

The seasons change as six months go by and he notices a boat that has not moved a lick since he began work. It's a 42' 1992 Lagoon TPI sailboat. Overall, it's in super rough condition and could use A LOT of work. He goes to his boss and inquires further.

"It's been abandoned here for six years. You can have it for $1,000 if you get it the hell out of my marina."

The now-Captain Scott took the deal and began to refurbish and restore this once-exquisite sailboat. He gave it a deep cleaning, replaced the propeller, stripped most of the electrical as there was a quite a bit of exposed wire, and modified the living quarters.

While he restored the boat, his boss took him for little sailing adventures on a similar boat so he could learn the ropes. He learned how to navigate the ocean, operate the levers and pulleys that raise and lower the sails, the necessary sailing terminology, and even got a couple experiences in nasty storms.

During the process of the restoration, Nathan lived minimally and frugally, saving as much money as he possibly could. Thankfully, due to his young age, he had not accumulated too much stuff, and therefore, there wasn't much to get rid of. All of his belongings fit snugly aboard. His goal was to have a year or two of income saved up so that he could focus his efforts on self-liberational media (i.e. a YouTube channel, writing a book, etc.).

After a couple years of hard work, Libertas was ready to set sail and so was he. He charted his journey (southwards in the direction of Ecuador) and truly began his life as a vonuan.

And it was a good life. He soon learned that boat maintenance is time consuming and can be expensive, but he made it work. He chronicled his adventures in the form of self-liberational media. He was unable to afford the ridiculously expensive "High Seas" Internet, and opted instead to record a batch of podcasts each month and return to land to upload them. He utilized WordPress' "Schedule Post" function, which allowed him to keep his audience tuned into a steady stream of content. For paying subscribers, he even gave them an opportunity to sail with him; it's a great opportunity for him to fund his adventures and a reward well-worth paying for his listeners.

As he became more competent, he realized that he wanted to return to the statist-servile society less and less for import-export. He theorized about the possibility of somehow making himself more self-sufficient aboard Libertas. He thought about hauling some sort of a floating platform behind him which would be loaded with fresh, organic vegetables. After further consideration, he realized that was probably a no-go.

He recalled Rayo's discussion on something called "crypto-culture," or small, hidden patches of food which could be harvested. "What if I grow my own food on an uninhabited ocean island?"

So, he sailed around and found the ideal candidate. Now, he was able to provide 100% of his food himself – fresh vegetables on the island and fresh seafood from the ocean. As is the case with any vonuan, he became more and more competent as the years went on.

And, from his self-liberational media, he was recruiting people in droves to make radical lifestyle changes in pursuance of freedom. He learned firsthand the accuracy of an oft-said proverb: A rising tide raises all boats.

Making Money on the Open Ocean

It's worth making a few notes on ways to make money while sailing fulltime. Back in 1966, Kerry Thornley published a series of articles sharing the same title as the next section. That will be the source of most of this information.

For smaller boats, there aren't a whole lot of options. The few that come to mind are self-liberational media, digital nomadism, and consulting.

For larger boats, the options expand quite drastically. Thornley elucidates:

"Charter sailing tourists in colorful parts of the world…is a good way to make money while living at sea, but it is not the only way in which a large boat can serve as a tool of production. Simple freedom from police harassment for group activities – such as wild parties, clandestine political meetings, illegal medical operations – is a valuable condition which a boat captain can provide for a fee. In addition, he can run cargoes to out-of-the-way places unserviced by major shippers, provide transportation to escaping political refugees, and undertake speculative anti-State ventures – such as the smuggling of American cigarettes into Spain, where high tariffs make such operations, however dangerous, extremely profitable. Smuggling opportunities in a world of antilibertarian trade policies, in fact, are legion – one can take diamonds out of

Africa and South America, run arms to rebels in Cuba, land used auto and refrigerator parts in Mexico, bring gold into certain near-totalitarian countries where ownership of some is unlawful...all for life, liberty, and property."

Obviously, I would never advocate you do anything illegal; if you decide to pursue any of the above methods, you do so at your own risk and of your own accord.

There are even larger applications of this strategy which could bring in a substantial amount of money but carry a lot more risk. Let's run through a hypothetical example here, assuming that there is somehow a massively funded anarchist organization, The Maritime Misesians (TMM).

TMM, an anarchist organization of roughly 20 members made rich from digital currencies, see an opportunity for huge profit in the open ocean: a floating, mobile sovereign free port of sorts (see below). Governments have this tendency to regulate everything into oblivion, which halts innovation, increases the barriers to entry, and makes a previously affordable product or service exorbitantly expensive. There is no industry more applicable here than Big Pharma.

Imagine the possibilities of an unhampered, unregulated medical industry in the open ocean. Think revolutionary medical research, no taxes or regulations, and an actually affordable product.

So, TMM decide to buy a large, decommissioned aircraft carrier from the Navy (where else would you get one of those?) for $2.8 million (actual price of one for sale in 2016) and outfit it as a giant marketplace. To keep themselves out of the line of fire of nation-states, they take the following precautions:

- Nuclear weapons are banned from sale;
- The location of the aircraft carrier changes often, although always in international waters, 200+ miles off any established coast;
- The entrepreneurs place a limit on the amount of drugs able to be purchased and transported elsewhere. All the State has to do is CLAIM that confiscated drugs came from there and they'd be at risk to face the wrath of the State.

In addition to just being a marketplace, there are also medical research labs, medical operation rooms, a nightclub, and a luxurious restaurant. The two biggest difficulties TMM's face is: 1) nation-state interference, and 2) finding customers to patronize the aircraft carrier.

I present this example, more so as a thought exercise, rather than a serious suggestion; obviously, this isn't in line with "minimalist" sailboating. "We" likely won't see any of these come into fruition anytime soon. If you refer back to mean-time to harassment, something like this would certainly be H-level vonu – as far as I know, there's no way to "hide" an aircraft carrier. Higher risk, higher reward.

The Permanent Floating Voluntary Society

When I tell the story of Rayo, one of the first retorts I often receive is, "I don't want to live in isolation." For the most part, I don't either! But, it would be wise to begin your journey as a solo vonuan unless you already have a freemate, significant other, children, etc. Rayo provides some wise advice on the subject:

> "Many a man will say, and sincerely believe, that he wants to vonu just as soon as he finds "the right woman" or "the right group" to do it with, but he doesn't want to do it alone. However, how do you (and he) know that he can do it, until he does it for a substantial time? If he can't stand living alone – if he soon gets bored with himself – chances are he will soon get bored with you, too. So suggest that he do it alone for a year or so before trying to link up."

So, let's say you've been living aboard your sailboat for a year now and are loving it! What sort of possibilities exist for the "social" vonuan?

The answer? A mobile intentional community, or, as per the title, a permanent, floating, voluntary society. For those new to the concept, an intentional community can be defined as:

> "A planned community designed from the start to have a high degree of social cohesion and teamwork. The members...typically hold a common social, political, religious, or spiritual vision and often follow an alternative lifestyle."

Similar to a van nomad caravan, the idea is to still have the workings and culture of a small society: division of labor, labor specialization, the ability to pool together resources, etc.

You may be lucky enough to have a handful of families ready to set sail around the same time you are. If so, you've already got the fixings for this community to develop. If you are heading out solo, without any potential mates, then it may be a little more difficult, especially when it comes to the stringent philosophical requirements for a vonuan. Your pool of potential candidates shrinks.

Rayo discusses the advantages of this strategy in *Vonu: The Search for Personal Freedom*:

> "The voluntary floating association has some advantages over the free-hamlet-in-the-hills. Not only will anchors be lowered where State interference is minimal; the very mobility discourages intervention. For instance, State school officials seldom molest the children of transients. Another blessing for parents: the irrationalist-coercivist influence of "outside" peer groups and mass communication media is considerably reduced. Differences of objective and conflicts of personality, which may disrupt an immobile intentional community, are easily resolved; the dissenters weigh anchor. And a "community" can develop by easy steps and without formal direction; no would-be founder need acquire a large tract of land, uncertain as to market demand or the response of the State."

From the minimalist sailboating vlogs I follow, it seems that these associations tend to happen spontaneously. Hopefully you'll have similar luck.

In conclusion, minimalist sailboating is a terrific option for vonuans. It does have some additional hurdles compared to van nomadism, but the increase in freedom is quite substantial. Instead of driving on "government roads," you sail the High Seas, where there really is no government.

It's worth noting that sailing can be rather difficult. Here are some recommendations I'd make for someone interested in pursuing this lifestyle:

- **Test out the lifestyle before committing.** Life on the sea is a whole hell of a lot different than on land. I'd recommend taking a "hitchsailing" trip – it's hitchhiking, only on the water. It's actually a rather safe practice, especially if you coordinate it in the Facistbook group, "Sailboat Hitchhikers and Crew Connection." Many of those folks know each other and can vouch for other members. It's worth noting the importance of making sure you're compatible with the captain and his crew (if applicable). You don't want to be stuck in close quarters with folks you can't stand – it might sully your experience.
    - o   www.facebook.com/groups/sailboatyacht
- **Take your time and do your homework.** The ocean can be a tranquil, enjoyable experience, but it can also be quite treacherous. The idea is self-liberation, not accidental suicide.
- **Be willing to pay** an experienced captain to teach you the ways of sailing. I don't know how much it costs, but I guarantee it's cheaper than going out as a novice and sinking a boat or worse.

"The floating voluntary society beings with a population of one." Will you set sail for sunnier waters?

Chapter 9: Perpetual Traveling

In a panarchistic sense, governments around the world compete with each other for tax cattle. They'll offer different incentives, tax breaks, and additional "privileges," such as marijuana decriminalization or gun ownership, to convince individuals to relocate to their jurisdiction. Sure, the ideal situation would be no affiliation with the world's most "successful" mass murderer known as government, but again, vonu is based on reality, not on how "we" as vonuans WISH things to be. That's the prerogative of the political crusaders.

As Rayo said, "Become internationally mobile. Stop being a 'captive audience' for the real life black comedies of a particular gang of clowns-turned-goons and begin making real market choices between States."

It is true that van nomadism and minimalist sailboating, generally speaking, are methods of perpetual traveling, but it's worth expanding upon the subject further. There are a couple of different applications to examine, but we should cover a few preliminary notes first: residential taxation, territorial taxation, and The Five Flag Theory.

Residential taxation is a bitch and is a major reason why many expats rescind their United States citizenship. Reason being, the IRS claims taxes on ANY money you make, regardless of whether it's in Spain, Antarctica, Mars, or anywhere else in the Milky Way Galaxy.

Territorial taxation on the other hand, means that you only owe "your" government of residence income tax if you make money inside their jurisdiction.

So, what is The Five Flag Theory? It's a way for an individual to not be considered a legal resident of any of the countries they spend time or operate in, and therefore, is a way to avoid the legal obligations that come with it. The "flags" are as follows:

1. **Passport and citizenship** in a country that does not tax money earned outside the country or attempt to control actions outside of its jurisdiction.
2. **Legal residence** in a tax haven.
3. **Business base** where one earns money, ideally somewhere with low corporate tax rates.
4. **Asset haven** where one keeps their money, ideally somewhere with low taxation of passive income and capital gains.
5. **Playgrounds** where one spends money, ideally somewhere with low consumption taxes.

This is the most popular strategy perpetual travelers use. Let's take a look at a couple of case studies to see how this lifestyle could be developed.

Case Study: Victor the Vagabond

Victor Cruz was born in Canada in the mid-70s. He worked as a developer in the technology realm for 20 years until the boom of the Internet. He started a couple online businesses and made a bunch of money in short order. He'd always wanted to live a life of travel but had never possessed the funds to do so. Now, he could.

Victor sold his house and all of his belongings, sans what he could fit into a suitcase. He did some research into what countries he might like to utilize for The Five Flag Theory and got his new legal affairs in order.

He traveled around for a while getting a feel for different countries to see where he would like to spend most of his time. He found that France, Ecuador, and Brazil were his absolute favorite places, but most countries only allow tourists to remain there for so long without applying for a tourist visa. Well, considering he's a perpetually traveling vonuan, he always relocates before having to go through that process.

He finds that he typically rents housing wherever he goes. Sure, he may not be building equity, but it beats the hell out of paying a ton of taxes each year. Since he flies everywhere, he does have a few run-ins a year with the airport bludgies. He dislikes the invasions of privacy and the coercion, but he feels it's a price worth paying to live the life that he truly wants to live.

Case Study: Winfred the Wanderer

Winfred was your average individual in the servile society just a few years ago. He was stuck at a dead-end job in Wellington, New Zealand, making just enough money to survive. His rent was high and he felt trapped in a life that he couldn't even recognize anymore. His life wasn't even his own. Out of desperation, he began doing some research on the Internet and stumbled across the van dwelling section of YouTube. He was enthralled with the lifestyle and decided that it was for him. So, he saved up as much money as he could, bought a van, and converted it into a live aboard rig.

Since he was already living frugally out of necessity before this change was quite smooth for him and allowed him to FINALLY save a substantial amount of money. He lived in his van working the same job for a handful of years while building up his investment capital. He eventually had enough to break free — he quit his job, sold his van, and flew to America.

For a few weeks, he stayed at an AirBnB in Austin, Texas until he found a new van to buy and convert. He traveled across North America for about a year and decided it was time to move on again. So, he sold the van and hopped on a flight to Perth, Australia, only to repeat the process.

When he was in Australia, he became enamored with a woman who lived aboard her boat, and she with him. They only spent a few weeks together before they decided to set sail to circumnavigate the globe. It would turn out to be a five year adventure and they loved every minute of it.

Now Winfred is free and he found another self-liberator in the process. He was willing to make the sacrifices necessary for a life of freedom. It wasn't easy, but nothing worthwhile in life really is. His case study is a great example of how a vonuan can use van nomadism as an intermediate vehicle for self-liberation (pun intended).

Advantages and Disadvantages

From the above case studies, you should be able to see some clear advantages, as well as disadvantages. Let's start with the advantages.

If you're a resident of a place you never spend time in, the politics at play are completely irrelevant. It'd be akin to caring about the politics of Italy after you take a weeklong vacation to Rome. Compared to your average news junkie, this opens up a lot of time for other pursuits; it'll probably save you some healthcare bills down the road, too (if you've made it this far in the book, politics probably makes your blood boil).

Perpetual travelers also have the ability to utilize legal interstices that aren't available to most stationary dwellers. They can organize their life in such a manner so as to avoid most of the coercion of the servile society; because, let's face it, the most coercion comes from the government presiding over your country of residence.

One other advantage was elucidated by Rayo. He said:

"The mobile libertarian not only bypasses most existing State coercion, but is well equipped to escape incipient totalitarianism. With the American government readying plans for general forced labor, rationing and censorship in the event of war or other "national emergency," escape can be essential for philosophical if not physical survival. And while a retreat in the boondocks can serve as a temporary hideout, when total fascist-socialism comes, those who fare best are usually those who leave early."

With the modern political climate and all this talk about a wall, I think Rayo's words are more important now than they even were then. After all, government walls are not meant to keep people out; they are meant to keep people in. History has more than borne out this fact. In this event, perpetual travelers will already be ahead of the game, as there are really no sane reasons they would ever choose America as their country of residence.

Unfortunately, there are some disadvantages though.

Most importantly would be this strategy's reliance upon "slave tags," only in this case, it's a passport, not necessarily a driver's license.

As Rayo so astutely points out, "Get a passport, but don't depend on it; passports may be revoked in the event of a 'national emergency'."

Earlier this year even, the American government revealed that they might suspend passports for "seriously delinquent" taxes, or, more specifically, in excess of $50,000 (including interest and penalties – those can add up QUICK). What's scarier is the fact that passports may be needed at some point in the near future to even travel domestically. Talk about a great way to keep the tax cattle in the cage.

Anyways, what does this mean for perpetual travelers? As I said above, I don't think any intelligent vonuan perpetual traveler would ever choose America as their place of residence – it's counter-intuitive to the entire notion of perpetually traveling. Furthermore, even if the individual in question "took pleasure" in paying taxes and didn't rescind their citizenship, it would be unwise to rely upon just an American passport. Imagine if you were in Costa Rica, about to board a plane and your passport was revoked for whatever reason (i.e. delinquent taxes, national emergency, etc.). I wouldn't want to be in that position.

A solution to this problem is dual citizenship and having two different passports (but, do your research and make sure most countries will accept it; for example, you probably wouldn't want to get a passport from Somalia or Afghanistan). That way, if one is revoked, you aren't shit out of luck in some foreign country. It's not a perfect solution and proposing citizenship for two countries to vonuans might be a tough sell, and rightfully so. Keep in mind, proper preparation prevents piss poor performance – try not to get stuck in Costa Rica (unless you want to, of course!).

Perpetual traveling is another interesting strategy for freedom pioneers and again, it's all up to you how you structure it. You could be Victor the Vagabond, Winfred the Wanderer, a combination of the two, or something all of your own.

Let's close out this section with some more timeless words from Rayo:

> "So, the free-man-of-the-world, like the alert shopper who buys the specials at various stores, selects the best features of various States. And his very mobility gives added protection from the worst depredations."

Chapter 10: Stationary Intentional Communities

In the 1990s, Hakim Bey coined the terms and developed the two concepts, permanent autonomous zones (PAZs) and temporary autonomous zones (TAZs). PAZs can be defined as:

"A community that is autonomous from the generally recognized government or authority structure in which it is embedded."

In other words, it's a recognition that the PAZ is located within the alleged jurisdiction of a government, yet it's a declaration that "inside this zone, we are autonomous."

Intentional communities of any flavor would be considered autonomous zones, yet the mobility of the vonu home base (the place where you are most invulnerable to coercion) is the determining factor as to whether the zone in question is temporary or permanent. For this section, we will focus on the stationary intentional community, in contrast to the mobile ones we examined in previous chapters: van nomad caravans and minimalist sailboat fleets. Rayo describes these PAZs as:

"...a smaller and more limited approach based on physical congregation of libertarians in a geographical area. The essential difference between an intentional community and a sovereign free port is admissions requirements – the intentional community would be smaller, less involved in external trade, not possess legal sovereignty, and require less capital."

To hammer this point in again, **if the coercers can find you, they can coerce you**. And in the case of this strategy, the bludgies will know EXACTLY where your community is located. This is the main drawback to PAZs, as mobility is what provides the highest degree of vonu. The community will also be expected to pay property taxes and ensure that they are abiding by local ordinances/codes or else face an escalation in coercion.

Another disadvantage arises due to the fact that this is a permanently fixed location; that is, human conflict. Recall the permanent, floating, voluntary association discussed above. If John had a major, **major** disagreement with Jane, all either of them has to do is weigh anchor and go on their merry way. With the permanent intentional community, though, there's too much at stake to simply walk away. John and Jane may each have a substantial amount of capital invested in the land, in addition to the time and effort spent on developing it for, say, a permaculture farm. Not a great situation.

All of that said, it doesn't mean this strategy should be tossed out, it just means that interested vonuans must be more creative in how they go about it.

So, if you're committed and this is what you're working towards, how can you ensure the success of your intentional community? Well, unfortunately, there's no way to "ensure success," but there are some things you can do to mitigate the risks.

First off, location, location, location. It probably wouldn't be wise to choose California, New York, Kabul, or any other extremely coercive or dangerous state. You should take into account: weather/climate, population, legal interstices you can utilize, the different governments presiding over the jurisdiction in question (local, county, state), nearest cities of any size for import-export, the terrain, average going prices for land, and, maybe most importantly, whether or not the area is incorporated or unincorporated. If it's unincorporated, you **should** avoid having to deal with nuisance abatement, allowing the possibility of going completely off-the-grid.

I'd also recommend that all members of this community be knowledgeable on security culture. After location, this is definitely the most important step – this could be the deciding factor as to whether your community flourishes or dies. All it takes is one slip up for the bludgies or private coercers to crash the party.

For example, let's say Alvin met a guy named Bill and they became friends; Alvin filled Bill in on the community but didn't disclose the location. What should Alvin do at this point? Well, what he SHOULD do is properly vet Bill to ensure that he's not a bludgie, bullshitter, or an otherwise incompatible individual. Let's say he doesn't do this and it turns out Bill's a bludgie trying to infiltrate the community. Let's also hypothetically say that there was some black/grey market activity happening in his line of sight. It's safe to say Bill would take this report back and a big heap of coercion would likely be on the way.

Lastly, I'd recommend a way to handle conflicts that may arise, likely some sort of an internal dispute resolution system that is agreed to explicitly by all members. I'm not sure if intentional communities in the past have done this, but I feel this is one way to ensure long-term viability of such a venture.

So, what sort of folks might be interested in starting a stationary intentional community? Rayo believes that:

> "The intentional community approach appeals to individuals who foresee an impending political-economic collapse and/or would like to try their hand at self-sufficient living. To others it might be of value as a vacation spot, or as a "bedroom community" where they could raise children away from many of the irrational influences prevalent in a philosophically "mixed" society."

Those would certainly be the advantages of this strategy, in addition to the fact that you would be living 100% of the time with like-minded individuals who truly understand the notion of self-ownership and respect your autonomy.

In conclusion, the disadvantages outweigh any potential advantages of this strategy, at least in my humble opinion. Yet, this is still something that individuals may wish to pursue. Take your time, do your research, and take special care in choosing who you will be living with.

Chapter 11: Vonuing in Cities

According to the 2010 U.S. Census Bureau, 80.7% of Americans live in urban areas. Many likely do so by choice, but others do so as a requirement for employment, or even possibly other reasons (e.g., knowing no other lifestyle or not being comfortable with living in any other location). Clearly then, some vonu lifestyle changes may not be appealing or possible for many folks. The question to ask then becomes, "Is it possible to vonu in cities?"

This topic is one that Rayo did not spend much time on, at least in the publications that I've been able to acquire. In Vonu: The Search for Personal Freedom, he wrote a two-page, ~800 word article on it, but that's it. So, this is one strategy that we will have to develop almost in its entirety for The Vonu Podcast. This section should be considered an introduction to the strategy at best with more extensive follow-up after further thought, consideration, and brainstorming.

Rayo highlighted five different approaches to vonuing in cities, namely:

1. Anonymity

2. Gather with fellows into a "ghetto"
3. A blend of concealment and deception
4. A den or camouflaged camp on unowned land, such as a "public park"
5. Van nomadism with city squat spots

We'll cover each of these separately.

Anonymity

Regardless of whether or not you're living in a city, a vonuan should ALWAYS exercise security culture when entering the statist-servile society. If you're living there full-time, then it's doubly important. Practicing the grey man is absolutely crucial. As Rayo advises, "Be visible but not noticeable. Conform outwardly while doing your own thing in secret. Be inconspicuous."

Remaining anonymous is becoming more and more difficult as time goes on, especially after 9/11. Many of the suggestions Rayo and other vonuans made are largely irrelevant, for example, "Renting under a nom de plume." That is certainly not possible today – most rental companies require a background and credit check, both of which require your social security number. Even if you're simply selling some old video games to Mega Replay, personally identifiable information (i.e. a driver's license) is almost always required for anything.

And for some vonuans, remaining anonymous is simply not enough. Rayo explicates:

"For me anonymity alone was unsatisfactory because of city psychological pressures. I was immersed in an alien culture with values hostile to my own. Whether or not I was especially vulnerable, I felt vulnerable."

The city psychological pressures are definitely one of the biggest obstacles to overcome when vonuing in cities. Not only can it be mentally "taxing" and exhausting being surrounded by statists all the time, but these pressures often pull once dedicated freedom pioneers back to submissive, conventional lifestyles. As of 1972, Rayo and others didn't really have any solutions to this. As of today, I really don't either. If you do, please let me know.

Gather With Fellows Into A Ghetto

This might be the strangest recommendation Rayo proposes in his book, so much so that I really don't have much to say about it. I'll let him explain it for you:

"A way to reduce psychological pressures is to gather with fellows into a "ghetto" – a second approach to city vonu. One loses anonymity with respect to the larger culture as one develops subculture speech, customs, mannerisms and dress. But one becomes a relatively indistinguishable member of the subculture, requiring that any organized aggressor attack everyone or no one. "All (Chinese, Niggers, Hippies...) look alike." This doesn't always stop aggressors – witness Jews in Nazi Germany, Japanese in U.S. The recommendations made by Walt Hayward presume ghettos of like-minded people...Ghettos are also possible in rural areas. The Takilma area southeast of Cave Junction, Oregon, is almost a "freek" ghetto. While freeks may not be in the majority yet, there are enough to render the area unattractive for anti-freeks, causing most land up for sale to be bought by freeks, etc. – analogous to what happens in new Black ghettos in cities. How much protection this provides remains to be seen. There have been quite a few arrests for growing/using pot, etc. A bigger crunch will come when substantial numbers of freek children become old enough for slave school. (Will the "Supreme Court" require long-hairs and short-hairs to be intermixed by bussing? Or will it compel kids to cut their hair middle length, with the length set by the majority vote every four years?)"

I suppose it's one way to surround yourself with like-minded people, but like Rayo, I'm quite skeptical of the proposition. If the bludgies were trying to shut this down in the 1970s, this is probably a lifestyle they wouldn't tolerate today; that, and do you really think there are enough vonuans interested in this to make it viable? It's probably as likely as the State being abolished tomorrow.

A Blend of Concealment and Deception

This is one of the most practical and realistic approaches Rayo presents. The idea is to "construct hidden, sound-proofed apartments and workshops beneath or within an 'owned' building ostensibly used for other purposes." For example, let's say that John is a vonuan who works as a mechanic and that he has his own shop. He could construct a hidden apartment within that would only be accessible by him and that only he would have knowledge of.

Rayo also notes that "such chambers could be blast, fire, and fallout resistant" and that it "offers some protection against...day-to-day predation." Another example of a hidden bedchamber can be found in the terrific crypto-agorist novella, #agora.

What are some considerations to take into account for someone interested in this blend of concealment and deception? Firstly, it's important to conceal the fact that you are going to be constructing anything – nosy neighbors or bludgies might inquire further. Also, think carefully about how you will enter and exit the premises, whether you decide upon a false wall, a hidden staircase underneath tiled floor, or whatever else. The idea is to avoid heavy foot traffic that could be picked up on by the bludgies or other coercers.

The disadvantages for this strategy are similar to the ones discussed in the anonymity section above. The city psychological pressures would still be an obstacle with little or no solution(s) at this time, in addition to the fact that even constructing this hidden bedchamber would be complicated.

This approach has some potential but it needs to be developed upon. Consider brainstorming on it and help come up with a way to make it practical.

Build A Den or Camouflaged Camp on Unowned Land

This specific approach is actually quite similar to wilderness vonu, the main difference being that this den or camp would be located in a "public" park inside a city. There is only one real advantage to this strategy which is easier access to the city. Other than that, this one is riddled with problems and obstacles. Of course, concealing your structure in a "public" park is going to be far more difficult than concealing a polyethylene a-tent in the Siskiyou National Forest. As with the other approaches, there are "general hazards of city living including smog and nuclear threat."

This strategy has actually been tested, though, and with short and long-term success. In Preform-Inform, it was reported that "a man built a shack and lived undetected for 17 years in a Portland city park. One of my colleagues from the UK recently sent me an image of a tent, right out in the open, located on public land. He informed me that it had been there, unmolested, for a few weeks (obviously, this individual in question was NOT practicing concealment).

It's worth noting that it would be wise to develop concealment skills in remote areas, so as to get experience without the higher risk of harassment by the bludg. Once you develop your competency in the wilderness, then you can opt for better city access.

Van Nomadism with City-Squat Spots

This is an approach that we already touched upon in Chapter 6, and is successfully practiced EVERY single day, all over the world. There is so much self-liberational media walking you through exactly how to do it and what considerations to take into account it's not even funny.

Some individuals choose van nomadism for this purpose alone, as it still provides them access to the city and their place of employment. Rayo elaborates on how to successfully stealth camp:

> "'Private' land, such as backyards of friends, is probably safer than streets for long stays. The vehicle need not be as self-contained since utilities are close at hand. Off-the-road performance isn't important. Appearance, conventionality, license plates, etc., are important."

A few other squat-spots that you might consider:

- **Walmart Parking Lots**: Walmart has always catered to RV'ers and travelers, but this possibility seems to be on its way out. Reason being, local governments are passing ordinances saying it's illegal to sleep in parking lots. That said, some van nomads still do it, but it's recommended to only sleep there one night at a time.

- **Hotel Parking Lots**: There are almost always vehicles in hotel parking lots, meaning that if you have a stealth van, you'll likely be able to get a night's rest without issue.

- **Mechanic Shops**: This one is a bit more risky, but it is a potential option. Obviously, there are always cars being worked on at mechanic shops, many of them remaining in the lot overnight. You might have luck sleeping there, as long as you're up early and gone before they open.

I'll leave it there for now and will point you in the direction of YouTube: just search for "Stealth Camping" and you'll be provided with plenty of results.

In summation, it's extremely important that this strategy be developed. Many folks are truly stuck in the city for whatever reason, but that doesn't mean they are unable to practice vonu. Sure, it may be more difficult in some ways, but keep in mind, vonu is not an all-or-nothing thing, nor is it black and white. Examine your current lifestyle and your goals, in addition to what it would take to get from where you are to where you want to be. Then, make a plan and execute it.

Chapter 12: Far-Out Vonu Strategies

Obviously, the entire purpose of this book is to give you, the reader, practical strategies to increase your personal freedom. That said, there are a couple H-level MTH options Rayo proposed that are unlikely to come to fruition in "our" lifetime: sovereign free ports, a libertarian country, seasteads, and spacesteads.

Along with these distant possibilities comes a colored history of libertarianism that most ideological adherents are not familiar with. In August of 2017, I wrote up that history for Ocean Living Magazine, the magazine of The Marinea Project (now defunct), which I was the communications specialist for.

SEASTEADING CASE STUDIES: LEARNING FROM THE FAILED ATTEMPTS OF THE PAST

For thousands of years, land has provided human beings the optimal headquarters for living. Resources were aplenty, large amounts of "real estate" were available for homesteading, and individuals could develop it as they saw fit.

That is, until two important things happened. One, the advent of urbanization, or the corralling of large amounts of people into small areas and, two, the various governments' jurisdictional claims to 99.9% of all land in the world, including the most obscure, uninhabited islands.

A large number of folks' subjective preferences lead them to remain in the cities, but there are those seeking a "return to the land" in the form of off-grid homesteading—they just want to be left alone with nature. But, governments tending to be the control freaks that they are, have a nasty habit of fining and evicting private property owners via nuisance abatement (i.e. local codes and ordinances).

As Tom Marshall (Rayo), a freedom pioneer in the 1960s and 70s said, "Apply your free market principles by setting sail for sunnier waters."

And he was right—the "homesteading" of the sea (seasteading) will play (and is playing) an inevitable role in the future of human freedom and survival.

Marinea is but one such project looking to found a village at sea; the other one with any notoriety would be The Seasteading Institute. Little known, there were also a few attempts at founding new libertarian countries in the open ocean in the mid-20thcentury.

For purposes of historical relevance, as well as potential lessons for current and future seasteaders, let's take a look at their failed efforts to see where they went wrong.

(Author's Note: Due to the scarcity of resources at the time this article "goes to press", specific years may not always be provided. The resources referenced are: "The Nation Builders' Struggle", Brian Doherty's "Radicals for Capitalism", Rayo's "Vonu: The Search for Personal Freedom", Roy Halliday's "Operation Atlantis", Erwin Strauss' "How to Start Your Own Country", and some updates on the projects from Wikipedia.)

The Free Isles Project

The Free Isles Project was a venture that spawned out of the Preform-Inform movement and the Innovator libertarian zine in the 1960s. The goal was to conduct research on the efficacy of setting up a new libertarian country, solutions to potential obstacles, and the seemingly endless possibilities if it were to come into fruition.

This project continued for a handful of years, but it never got past the talking stage. Eventually, the movement subsided after disagreements arose regarding the size and scope of government, the lack of individuals willing to become involved, and the potential ramifications from existing nation states.

Nonetheless, the Free Isles Project seems to be the origin of these ventures and influenced at least one, if not all, of the projects below.

Operation Atlantis

From the outset, the Free Isles Project was just a research effort. The first actual attempt at bringing a new libertarian nation into fruition was Werner Stiefel's Operation Atlantis.

The plan was laid out in three stages: "(1) gather libertarians in a single location, (2) acquire an ocean vessel and declare it to be an independent nation while in international waters, and (3) create 'an artificial island as close to the shores of the U.S. as international law will permit and Uncle Sam will tolerate.'"

Furthermore, according to Brian Doherty in his book, Radicals for Capitalism, their goal was to "eventually obtain sovereignty over some island…and turn it into a fresh new country." From there they would have their base of operations and would start to build artificial platforms which would hopefully coalesce into the actual objective—a floating nation on the water.

The location he chose for recruiting libertarians was a hotel he had purchased in Saugerites, New York, which is right on the Hudson River, giving them water access to the Atlantic Ocean.

From scratch, they constructed a boat out of rebar and cement and set sail, only to have their vessel tip over and catch fire in the Hudson River. Persevering, they were able to navigate the vessel to the Silver Shoals area (near the Bahamas) when their ship sank.

Luckily, Steifel had already negotiated a 220-year lease for some land on the Haitian island, Tortuga, with the agreed-upon reason being for a small commercial chemical-mixing plant. But, once the Haitians learned of their plan to start a floating nation (**from their own publication**), President Jean-Claude Duvalier drove them out of the area, as it had already been slated for other purposes.

It is reported by Erwin Strauss, author of How to Start Your Own Country and visitor to the hotel, that "Mr. Stiefel was approaching the enterprise as a Sunday afternoon diversion," while focusing most of his time and effort on his pharmaceutical company. Strauss attributes that as one of the many reasons the dream of Atlantis died.

Michael Oliver's, "The Capitalist Country"

Michael Oliver was a Lithuanian-born concentration camp survivor who set out to found "The Capitalist Country" in 1968.

He investigated many areas for his new nation and attempted to solidify purchases of land from countries with little government, but it was to no avail until Minerva was founded in 1972. Oliver and his crew laid claim to "two small coral atolls in the South Pacific, 400 miles south of Fiji," and 260 miles northeast of the Kingdom of Tonga. Notices were sent to nations and they began dredging, capping out at 15 acres before running out of investment capital—far below their goal of 2,500 acres.

Doherty reports that the "project was breaking apart over personal squabbling" and that "…Oliver was washing his hands of the whole thing."

Surrounding island countries caught wind of the venture and understood the negative ramifications if it were allowed to succeed. Then, on February 23, 1972, a box of supplies was dropped, labeled, "supplied and maintained by the government of Tonga." The actions by the Tongan government were supported by many surrounding island countries. And, in the blink of an eye and with one gun boat, Minerva was conquered by the king of Tonga.

After that, Oliver pursued other strategies in founding his nation until he finally returned to the original goal—building artificial ocean cities. In the early 1990s, he set out to found the country of Oceania and penned the venture as the already known and nostalgic Atlantis Project.

In less than a couple of years it ended and at oceania.org it still reads:

"The Atlantis Project, which proposed the creation of a floating sea city named Oceania, began in February 1993, receiving nationwide publicity from The Art Bell Show, Details Magazine, The Miami Herald, Boating Magazine, and worldwide publicity in Canada, New Zealand, Hong Kong, England, and Belgium. The project ended in April of 1994."

Sea City "Taluga"

In 1969, the Cortez Development Corporation set out to found Sea City Taluga, a project focused primarily on tourism and recreation, rather than libertarian ideals like the previous case studies. Nonetheless, they still planned on setting up an autonomous government, albeit structured more like a corporation's board of trustees than a traditional one.

The location chosen was Cortez Bank, an area allegedly claimed by no government 100 miles west of Mexico. In the most complete article written on the subject of new libertarian nations, John L. Snare claims that, "The bank rises from the deep ocean floor and is not on the continental shelf by any accepted geological or legal definition."

Phase 1 was estimated to cost $350 million (keep in mind the year) and the entire project a substantial $2 billion—it was a MAJOR undertaking.

But, unfortunately, sometime after 1972, the U.S. government declared that the bank, as part of the continental shelf, was US territory. The plan died and all capital investment in the project was wasted.

What Can We Learn?

Let's first revisit why these projects failed or came to an end:

- The Free Isles Project: It was purely a research venture and the participants deemed it to be an inefficacious pursuit.
- Operation Atlantis: It seems they weren't completely honest in their contractual agreement with Duvalier, and therefore, he drove them out of the area when they started work on the floating nation.
- Operation Minerva: Their fate was sealed by infighting, a lack of funding, and an embarrassing lack of defense.
    - Oceania/Operation Atlantis II: It was simply a lack of funding and interest.
- Sea City Taluga: The US caught wind of the project and declared the continental shelf US territory.

Two terms need to be defined to make sense of this:

- Contiguous Zone (CZ): A band of water extending from the outer edge of the territorial sea up to 24 nautical miles (27.6 miles) from the baseline, within which a state can exert limited control for the purpose of preventing or punishing infringement of its customs, fiscal, immigration or sanitary laws and regulations.

- Exclusive Economic Zone (EEZ): Extends from the outer limit of the territorial sea to a maximum of 200 nautical miles (230.2 miles) from the territorial sea baseline…A coastal nation has control of all economic resources within its exclusive economic zone…However, it cannot prohibit passage or loitering above, on, or under the surface of the sea.

The demise of Operation Atlantis can easily be attributed to the fact that they were within the CZ of Haiti and that their contractual agreement, as far as we know, did not include their plans for starting a nation at sea.

Operation Minerva ("The Capitalist Country") provides us with a more sinister outcome. They were well outside the EEZ of Fiji and were about 30 miles outside of the EEZ of Tonga, yet, the Tongan government still brought forth aggressive action to evict Oliver and his associates, much to the satisfaction of the surrounding island nations.

Erwin Strauss attributes their downfall to their lack of ability to defend their land, yet he postulates that Tonga could have easily obtained military support from the larger nations if it was necessary. To paraphrase Psalms, put not your trust in princes, nor should you place faith in governments to actually follow their own laws.

Moreover, Sea City Taluga provides us with an example of what not to do—utilize any continental shelf, lagoon, atoll, etc. that is within the EEZ of the United States. Even though Snare claimed that there is no legal or geological justification for "ownership," the U.S. still swooped in and crashed the party. It's not wise to put that much investment capital at risk when the government can change terms and definitions willy-nilly.

How Marinea Plans to Avoid These Issues

The Cay Sal Bank is well outside any nation or country's CZ, and Marinea will not be "infringing" upon any nation or country's EEZ, since it will be a floating village at sea. Also, the success of Marinea will not depend or rely upon some contractual agreement with the government of the Bahamas nor of any other country. There will be neighborly cooperation, if applicable, but that's about it.

Furthermore, the three phase plan is realistic and doesn't require hundreds of millions of dollars of investing to get off the ground. The first phase of the project specifically will be a ship under flag of convenience by way of a modified shipping barge. The efficacy of this strategy has been proven time and time again.

Summarily, one of the issues that continually came up with the aforementioned case studies, as well as other "new nation" projects, is the lack of or running out of funding. Marinea has an answer to this problem. Once phase one is achieved, there will be extensive money-making possibilities which will reduce (if not eliminate) the need for outside investing.

Conclusion

As George Santayana is attributed to have said, "Those who do not learn from history are doomed to repeat it." Current and future seasteaders would be wise to learn from the mistakes of their predecessors and correct them to increase their chances of success.

In the long view of human history, this is still a brand new strategy and I envision many more unforeseen obstacles before the inevitable success. Seasteaders are the pioneers of the modern era—rather than utilizing the failed political means, they are the folks seeking to shift the entire paradigm and open the world up to a whole new slew of possible solutions to problems that humans face going into the future.

~~~

So, as you can see, there were quite a few attempts by libertarians to setup free countries, sovereign free ports, and other seastead ventures, but, for one reason or another, they all failed. They are worth discussing though, because if any of these were to be successful, the game would change.

You can probably already think of a few advantages of such strategies, but here's what Rayo had to offer:

"The most ambitious scheme for a local area of freedom so far proposed, a sovereign free port would potentially have much to offer. The "free isle" resident would (hypothetically) have all of the advantages of participating in world commerce while being free from taxes and regulations. Furthermore, a "free isle", if it were successful, could be a very effective demonstration of the merits of laissez-faire capitalism."
~~~

There are different variations of the above strategies. Let's examine those briefly.

- Libertarian countries could hypothetically be founded on uninhabited ocean islands, seasteads, or on land purchased from an existing government.
- Sovereign free ports could hypothetically be created on decommissioned aircraft carriers or otherwise large boats, underwater in a large submarine (why not?), or on land leased or purchased from an existing government (think Hong Kong).
- Seasteads could hypothetically be founded in international waters (like Marinea), outside the purview of any government, or in the jurisdiction of another country like The Seasteading Institute is pursuing with French Polynesia.

Obviously, not all approaches are created equal and I prefer the strategy in which there is no subjugation to governments — hell, from looking at the history, it's clear that they can't be trusted to keep their agreements, nor can they be relied upon to mind their own damn business and leave "us" peaceful people alone. But, "we" as vonuans already know that.

Fortunately, it appears some of the focus is shifting away from political crusading and there are modern attempts to bring any of these strategies into fruition. I mentioned The Seasteading Institute and The Marinea Project (unfortunately, now defunct due to a lack of funding and interest) a moment ago, but the newest attempt is by the Free Society Foundation. They are looking to purchase land from an existing government to be used as a new libertarian country.

I wrote an article on the latter previously.

ROGER VER, FREE SOCIETY FOUNDATION PLAN TO FOUND NEW LIBERTARIAN COUNTRY

[**Author's Note:** Surprisingly, I have found Roger's presentation at the Nexus Conference. He clarifies a couple of points of concern I address in the article. I will notate which portions in [brackets] below the original statement. Nonetheless, Erwin S. Strauss' concerns are still valid.]

Many strategies have been pursued by libertarians/anarchists over time to increase personal freedom and minimize the influence of States. One such strategy is the founding of a new libertarian country, wherein private property is respected and the efficacy of the free market can be proven once and for all.

The first such attempt that I have been able to come across was Preform-Inform, a group of southern California freedom seekers in the 1960s, who investigated the prospects of founding a new libertarian country on a floating artificial platform or on an uninhabited ocean island somewhere. After a handful of years, the members gave up, citing the many (to them) unsolvable obstacles.

Other such projects include Operation Atlantis, Michael Oliver's "The Capitalist Country," Sea City "Taluga," the Dupont-Caribbean Freeport Resort, and Oceania, all of which failed.

Roger Ver and the folks at the Free Society Foundation plan to do something similar and have allegedly already raised $100 million.

They claim that the solution "to really gain sovereignty…is to negotiate with an existing government" by outright buying a piece of land from them.

Their criteria for a location are: "proximity to existing economic powerhouses, accessibility by water, located in a safe, conflict-free area, stable existing government, nations with a significant national debt, a flexible constitution that allows granting sovereignty, [and] acceptable minimum size for the land."

As expected, the rule of law will be based on libertarian principles and free markets.

That all seems well and good, except for the fact that this has been tried before and to no avail. For example, Werner Steifel, the founder of Operation Atlantis, negotiated a 220-year lease for land on the Haitian Island, Tortuga, and not long after they settled, President Jean-Claude Duvalier expropriated the project once he discovered their plans.

Similarly, Dupont Caribbean Inc. of Texas made an agreement with the Haitian government to build a freeport-resort on the same island and Duvalier, again, expropriated the project, this time in favor of the Gulf Oil Corporation.

Not to mention, the founders (or, in some cases, CEO's), all scoured the Earth in search of a government that would sell them a piece of land and they had to settle on leases.

Erwin S. Strauss, the "authority" on new country projects in the 20th century, offers some valuable insight into the potentiality for a nation-state or country selling a piece of land to freedom seekers in his book, How to Start Your Own Country (1979). First off, he says:

> "One approach to avoiding the need for a military establishment…is buying the territory in question from the nation that currently has it…But this is basically a secondary matter, meaningless until the military situation has been provided for. If the new country lacks the willingness or ability to defend the purchased territory by force of arms, the selling country will have a strong incentive to repudiate the sale as soon as the purchaser's check clears…In any case, without being backed up by **force of arms**, any bill of sale or title deed held by the new country **would be a worthless scrap of paper**." pp. 11-12 [Emphasis added]

And it makes perfect sense. This strategy essentially puts the faith in the State to actually uphold their contractual agreement and to not do what they do best: use initiatory force. Consider a hypothetical, non-libertarian drug-dealer—if he can run away with the money **and** the drugs, why wouldn't he?

Although, let's take a step back—why would a nation-state or country even consider selling a portion of their land to freedom seekers? Chances are, they won't. Strauss continues:

> "The closest thing to a sale of sovereignty that is conducted routinely is the sale of corporation charters and ship registrations to all comers – with minimum strings attached – by tax-haven countries…But **any number of those can be sold without reducing the size of the country doing the selling**…once [the country] is sold, there is no further income to be had…" p. 12 [Emphasis added]

In other words, a country or nation has no financial incentive to actually sell a piece of their land when they can ensure continued payments via the aforementioned methods and even taxation, while still retaining sovereignty. I suppose if a country/nation was in such dire straits financially, maybe they would, but that first excerpt from Strauss comes into play — why wouldn't they just send their military to re-take it over, after the fact?

Strauss provides another interesting reason why countries are de-incentivized from selling pieces of their land to country builders:

"There is also the great-power influence… They have networks of grants-in-aid, favorable trade terms, military assistance programs, etc., to make it worth any small country's while to accommodate one or more of them. These great powers want to see the status quo maintained. Especially, **they want to see the number of countries held down**, because the fewer the players there are…the easier it is for the great powers to manage things to their own advantage." pp. 12-13 [Emphasis added]

So, small countries are even further dissuaded from selling off a portion of their land, since they could face potentially deadly ramifications from the great powers. And, the $100 million dollars Ver and the Free Society Foundation have to work with is likely a drop in the bucket considering how much stolen "aid" the great powers can provide.

Also consider the fact that there would be no vice crimes in AnCapistan, Libertopia, or whatever hypothetical free society. If it touched borders with an existing country or nation-state, you can guarantee there would be black marketeers running drugs, weapons, and other contraband into the abutting country.

[**Author's Update:** In his presentation, he says (paraphrasing) that there will be no smuggling of drugs or weapons into other countries for obvious reasons.]

The established country with tyrannical laws on the books would not be pleased with that prospect, and it would definitely be something they would take into account when deciding whether or not to sell land to country builders.

So, now that Strauss has probably put a damper on your day with reality, what solutions does he offer to make this solution more likely to be a success?

Well, to paraphrase Strauss, a significant enough military force would be required "to head it off [the threat], neutralize it, defeat it, turn it away, or otherwise insure that great-power intervention won't do them in."

Keep in mind that attacks from small countries aren't all the new country founders will have to concern themselves with — it's also the great powers that are always looking to advance their interests. To defend against that seems impossible — no new country would initially have the money or men to build a military to turn away the massively-funded nation-state armies, and no private security firm would be stupid enough (nor would they have the resources and manpower) to agree to such a job. Strauss proposes the solution:

> "Now, however, a new factor is entering the equation: **cheap weapons of mass destruction**…Even with these weapons, a small unit cannot expect to win outright a war with a large one. However, it can threaten **to inflict serious damage** on the large unit in the process…by promising to inflict grievous injury in the process of being crushed, they can give the larger units incentive to make detours around the smaller ones; to pursue their great-power interests somewhere else." p. 19 [Emphasis added]

As an anarchist, pondering that causes extreme uneasiness but Strauss is simply laying out the reality of the situation.

[**Author's Update:** In his presentation, Roger states that one of the limitations of this new Free Country will be no nuclear weapons; to paraphrase, he stated that nukes are a violation of the non-aggression principle because they can't be used for any deference purpose and it's a threat to a lot of innocent individuals.]

He continues:

> "Now, some new-country organizers will recoil at the thought of inflicting large numbers of casualties…But the fact is **that war**, and the inflicting of such number of casualties, lies **at the heart of statecraft**, and he who has no stomach for it needs to look for another line of work. The only way that a nation can avoid having to inflict such causalities is to convince all…that **it is ready and willing to inflict them…**" p. 19 [Emphasis added]

So, the recommendation is that new-country organizers first take steps to make or acquire weapons of mass destruction. If they don't, the chances of the libertarian free society surviving (or even coming into existence) are slim to none. It goes without saying that if any new country project decides to go this route, it must be done with the utmost secrecy. Remember when Iraq was **merely accused** of having WMD's? Keep it a secret.

Nonetheless, I wish Ver and the Free Society Foundation the best of luck. One of the major hurdles is funding; it appears they're off to a swell start there. Though, I sincerely hope the capital investment put into this project doesn't end up expropriated by a State, but we'll just have to see.

In summation, I truly am happy to see the focus moving away from political crusading into direct action-oriented strategies, even if they are unlikely to ever come into fruition.

But, that's not grounds for pessimism.

After continued failures, I do believe that individuals will decide to take steps themselves to increase their personal freedom, whether that take the form of van nomadism, intentional communities, minimalist sailboating, perpetual traveling, or whatever.

The outlook for personal freedom has never looked better.

~~~

Honestly, there is nothing I would love to see more than a functional, stable, new, floating libertarian country located out in international waters somewhere. I would be one of the first "settlers." Although, in my estimation, "we" are still quite far away. Reason being, the current model of nation-states is in no way conducive to this strategy. It will probably take the collapse of the concept (well, or at least just the collapse of America and the EU) as a whole, but even then, it sort of depends upon what comes next.

Although, on a smaller scale, I do think we may see some seasteads in the near future. Early on, they would be small; at most, maybe a dozen early entrepreneurs, self-liberators, or founders of the project in question. Import-export would still be necessary, as it would take some time for an alternative economy to develop. How long, you ask? How the hell am I supposed to know? A better question to ask is, "How many libertarians, anarchists, or other folks **would be willing and able to uproot their entire lives in an attempt to live on the**
~~~

open ocean?" That is the problem similar projects of the past faced and it is one that "we" will have to deal with going into the future.

There is one other strategy whose future is even more distant than the ones we've already covered. It is the setting and a plot device for many of the best anarchist/libertarian novels: of course, I am referring to spacesteading.

As I said above, if any of the aforementioned strategies were to be successfully implemented, a free society might actually exist in physical space and time. Well, if/when spacesteading comes into fruition, **governments become irrelevant.** Consider the opportunity cost of chasing tax delinquent, spacecraft nomads throughout the universe; also consider the time, money, and effort it would take for governments to locate and subsequently shut down stationary free societies in the vastness of space.

Sure, these may not be the most likely possibilities, but they are fun to think about.

Chapter 13: Conclusion

Rayo was right: "Freedom does indeed 'need' more full-time professionals; not collective-movement preachers seeking a coterie of followers, but explorers/inventors/developers of liberated life-ways."

Undoubtedly, numerous folks are truly seeking a way out of the statist-servile society, but they don't see any options outside of political crusading or apathy. Many are being emotionally and physically broken down by the 9-5 grind, the daily pressures of the servile society, and the recognition of how truly unfree they really are. That being the case, "our" task as vonuans now becomes self-liberation and marketing, in that order.

Reason being, if "we" are ever going to see an alternative economy, a sovereign free port, a new libertarian country, or whatever other grandiose strategy come into fruition, "we" need to first break people free from the servile society and into a lifestyle change of their choosing. Additionally, if "we" are ever going to see the abolition of the State, "we" must do our damnedest to eliminate the market demand for it; a great way to do that is by showing individuals that there are other options and to help them in the process as much as possible. Some entrepreneurs may even be able to monetize such a venture in the form of consulting or the development of tools or services to ease the transition from the First Realm to the Second Realm.

Rayo's first book, *Vonu: The Search for Personal Freedom*, was initially published in 1983. 35+ years later, many of these strategies are just as practical now as they were then, if not more so, thanks to the evolution of technology. Yet, some recommendations he and others posited are extremely outdated, destined to fail in the modern day. Vonu is based upon reality, not legality, and therefore, it will develop according to the external factors of the present time.

Freedom is not free. It takes time, effort, money, an extreme amount of dedication, and a willingness to make sacrifices; it requires the willingness and ability to create, develop, and to problem solve, as "we" are the self-liberators of the 21st century, pioneering the path forward to a freer future. It is not for everybody, and neither is vonu.

There's no better way to end this book than with these wise, timeless words from our friend and posthumous mentor, Rayo:

"A vonuan, to me, is not just someone living in a particular manner. Life-styles may change. A life-style which was vonu 100 years ago may not be vonu today; some life-styles vonu today were not possible 100 years ago and may not be vonu 50 years from now. A vonuan is someone who places a high value on relative invulnerability to coercion – someone for whom freedom is worth a fair amount (though not infinite) of effort, inconvenience, discomfort. To a vonuan, vonu is not just a means to other ends, nor is it an ultimate end – like most qualities of life, and life itself, it is both. A vonuan will choose whatever way of living offers personal sovereignty and will change life-style again and again if necessary."

Your free future is closer than you think.

Chapter 14: Bonus Content

1. An Answer To "The Omnipotence of State…"

There is little doubt that the State, the institution whose sole function is to **legitimately** coerce and inflict violence upon others, makes a dangerous enemy. One must only look at certain events of the 20th century to verify this fact, although a look at the entirety of human history would paint a similar picture: give a human being a position of great power, and inevitably, they will become the worst type of dictator in short order. Give thousands upon thousands of these men (and women) parasitic positions, and you have an entire institution of megalomaniacs.

Therefore, when examining the scope of human history, it's no surprise that many have a tendency to deify the State and give it god-like characteristics ("omnipotent," "omniscient," and "omnipresent"). While it's understandable, I will argue that this sort of mindset is not only unproductive for self-liberators, but that it is also untrue because the State is largely incompetent.

It's unproductive…

When it comes to self-liberation and alternative lifestyles, individuals in the statist-servile society (and even some anarchists, too) seem to always come up with an endless list of why such-and-such lifestyle is unpractical, unrealistic, unaffordable, crazy, downright stupid, or whatever. Considering the practicality of some of these lifestyles, it would seem to be the case that this reaction is a subconscious defense mechanism. Because, let's face it, human beings do inherently want to be free, but they tend to place as many barriers in the way as possible.

Some people love their chains; some need them; and folks like me are eleutheromaniacs (maniacs for freedom).

It reminds me of an article by Paul Rosenberg titled, 9 Reasons People Fear Freedom, from his book, A Lodging of Wayfaring Men. The first item on the list is fear of responsibility, and rightfully so. He writes:

"Freedom is threatening because it eliminates the possibility of shifting responsibility for your errors onto others. Freedom puts you right out in the open, with no cloak for your mistakes. It also gives you full credit for your successes, but that is seldom considered, as the fear-based impulses are generally stronger."

To be free, means to accept personal responsibility for your life and your actions. That prospect is daunting for many who have become brainwashed and propagandized to depend upon the State.

Similarly, I think this is another reason why some anarchists will elevate the State to this god-like status. Theists argue that God is here, has always been here, and will forever be here. So, if the State has been here forever and will continue to be here into infinity, then why the hell would "we" even try to fight it? Why even try to escape? Resistance is futile.

Even if the above were true, that mindset is abhorrent and unproductive; it's a retreat to apathy, it's an excuse for laziness, and it really eliminates most of the purpose from a self-liberator: if you will forever be a slave regardless of the actions you take, is life really worth living? Maybe, but that sounds a bit depressing to me.

For those who are freedom-minded but more so philosophically (i.e. Murray Rothbard), this sort of deification of the State leads them to believe that freedom can only happen in the long run, after enough minds have been changed. **"I can't be free until everyone else is free!"** With this controlled schizophrenia still largely intact, backsliding into political crusading is quite typical; sigh, Murray.

Unfortunately though, this mindset is quite predominant in the anarchist and libertarian community today; a bunch of people trying to philosophize their way to a free society. That alone will never be enough; theory and action are a necessary duality. This is the role vonu plays in the creation of a freer future. As Rayo said in *Vonu: Book 2 – Letters From Rayo*:

> "We may still have some contact with That society but we won't have to worry appreciably over what idiotic thing the people-molesters do next (any more than somebody who takes a vacation at the Riviera now and then needs to be much concerned about the politics of France.) Our change in life-style will be, in a sense, **an answer to the omnipotence-of-State line of Rothbard and Hess. We will answer not in words but by doing – the only real way.**" [Emphasis added]

THE STATE IS LARGELY INCOMPETENT…

Even the things the State is best at, it is still incompetent at to one degree or another. Take theft and lying as the State's most effective aspects.

- **Theft**: In 2013, the size of the underground economy was estimated at $2 trillion, or $500 billion in unpaid taxes. The large majority of those folks will never have any run-ins with the IRS; reason being, there are 10,000 IRS agents attempting to collect from 122 million American taxpayers.
- **Lying**: Now obviously, dishonesty is a requirement for a State to hold control and perceived legitimacy. If the modern State was 100% open with the way the system operated and why, "I believe there would be a revolution before tomorrow morning," to quote Henry Ford. And of course, they are incompetent at this; there are continuous leaks from former employees/contractors, hackers have been known to infiltrate their systems, etc. They can try to keep things a secret, but the truth always seems to find its way out.

So, they're quite incompetent, even at the things they are best known for doing.

Conspiracists also have a tendency to deify and bolster the State. For every single school shooting, bombing, or other terrorist attack, there's no shortage of individuals ready to claim that X, Y, and Z events were successful false flags, perfectly orchestrated by the State.

Now, I'm not saying there aren't real false flags; there certainly are and I've dug into quite a few in the past. What I am saying is that the State is probably more than happy to have some folks tossing blame their way for these events. If the perception is that they can orchestrate the Sandy Hook shooting and get away with it, fear and consternation are likely emotions, meaning they get to stay in power.

Therefore, it's no surprise that conspiracists often get stuck in the minarchist cage, rarely discussing solutions outside of politics. IF the State now has the attributes of God-like power and if it will be here forever, then the BEST "we" can hope for is a return to a smaller size.

Let's also consider the fact that 99% of government programs are complete and utter failures, at least when taken in context with the stated goal (i.e. wars on drugs, terror, crime, and poverty, the United States Postal Service, and the Department of Motor Vehicles, to name a few examples). Oh, the law of unintended consequences; that dreaded, economic principle that despicable central planners can never escape from. Do any of these things sound akin to "god-like characteristics"? I don't think so.

So, yes, the "omnipotence-of-State line of Rothbard and Hess" is riddled with issues. First, it's unproductive, and second, the State is largely incompetent, EVEN at the things it does best. Is it still a dangerous enemy? You bet your ass it is, and self-liberators should not ignore this fact. Rather, they should acknowledge their enemy exists, learn its strategies and tactics, and develop lifestyles to defend one's self against the threat of coercion.

And that's what vonu is. It is a coherent philosophy and strategy, and is your tool for self-liberation. Yes, Rayo, you're exactly right: "We will not answer in words but by doing – the only real way."

2. Pursuing Vonu: Handling Objections From the Servile Society

One reason why #vonu is such a radical freedom strategy is that it requires individuals to drastically alter the lifestyle they have been living. Most folks are NOT willing to do that, and therefore, the instinct (it seems) is to try to tear down and convince the self-liberator otherwise: that they should be "thankful" for being born here in "America" and that they are blessed to be able to pursue "The American Dream." Of course, I believe jealousy is a major part of that -- "If I can't be free, HE/SHE can't either."

Just more examples of the horizontal social control, or, in other words, slave on slave violence reinforcing the State and the statist-servile society.

What advice would I posit for dealing with this?

First off, don't let the criticisms or expectations from those in the #FirstRealm affect the plan you have for your pursuit of #vonu. In other words, don't feel "guilt," "shame," or whatever for living a lifestyle not approved by those in the servile society.

If you're a van nomad working a few half days a week, making little enough to not be liable for income theft, an individual may try to guilt you by accusing you off "freeloading" off the system. You know what I say to that person? Pardon my French, but fuck you. I didn't choose to be born here, I didn't setup this system, and I sure as hell don't consent to it. And I thought this was the "Land of the Free" anyways? Ha. Right.

My first piece of advice above may appear to go without saying, but it's critically important if one is going to be successful; consider it a milestone in exorcising those collectivist spooks. Similarly, recall Second Realm: Book on Strategy, namely number 8 of "Next Steps":

"Give up collectivist thought, especially asking for permission and requiring others to support you before you do anything."

Recognizing and managing your controlled schizophrenia is the crucial first step in pursuing vonu. Without it, vonu will likely NOT be a lifestyle change, but rather a foray with a return to a conventional lifestyle. In summation, as Rayo said:

"Whether one will be happier as a freeman or as a slave partly depends on the individual. But this choice is not open to most libertarians. Relative contentment in servitude is possible only for those who believe in it; most libertarians are too independent and well-informed. **For libertarians the choice is between freedom and neurosis.**" [Emphasis added]

So, what's it going to be? Freedom? Or neurosis?

Section III:
Updating Vonu

"Like it or not, everything is changing. The result will be the most wonderful experience in the history of man, or the most horrible enslavement that you can imagine. Be active or abdicate. The future is in your hands." -William "Bill" Cooper (1989)

Chapter 15: (Four Years Later) Vonu As A Philosophy & Freedom Strategy

Unlike many decades before, the practice of vonu is less a choice today, especially for those of us with lifestyles and perspectives drastically in variance with those of the servile society. This highly technological world is changing the dynamics of vonu, meaning that potential adversaries have expanded from the State and fascist corporations, to so-called artificial intelligence and adversarial hardware & software.

But while the eye of Babylon is seemingly becoming more omniscient, the opportunities to slip away into the darkness or to build a lifestyle largely invulnerable to coercion abound. Let's examine vonu as a philosophy and freedom strategy...four years later.

VONU IS YOURS FOR THE MAKING.

This is the philosophical essence of vonu, as well as its necessary action counterpart, all wrapped up in one short sentence. And to me, this is the true selling point of vonu:

That despite what is transpiring in the servile society, and regardless of what anyone else is doing, vonu enables the individual self-liberator to create their own liberated lifestyle.

This stands in stark contrast to the collectivist servile society, wherein, if you fall prey to the hive mind, you're probably going to end up sacrificing yourself to the borg. Vonu, on the other hand, requires the dispelling of such collectivist spooks.

So, individually speaking, things haven't really changed much in terms of vonu's philosophy and action – the committed freedom seeker can still successfully build a lifestyle resilient to rampant coercion.

In terms of communities or collectives though, there's some new developments to cover; but first, let's refresh ourselves on the main drawbacks with intentional communities/homesteads.

- The fixed location makes the vonuan more vulnerable to coercion;
- "Land ownership" opens up the vonuan to property taxes, nuisance abatement, and other interactions with State bureaucrats;
- Investment capital concerns: initially raising, and potentially losing

With those always in the back of my mind, the manufactured chaos kicked off in 2020, alongside the looming promises of food shortages (& more general supply chain issues), shutdowns, and the ramping up of technocratic totalitarianism vis-a-vis "immunity passports," to name a few.

My actions were somewhat sparked by fear, I will admit that, but taking into account Second Realm strategy, the picture started coming together.

In Second Realm strategy, there's an entrepreneurial role called the "proxy merchant." This individual facilitates interactions between the First and Second Realms. Some quick examples would be buying bitcoin from a miner (the proxy merchant) versus a privacy-hating exchange; or in this context, a trusted individual who will hold the land in their name and maintain interactions with the State.

Utilizing a proxy merchant is a good first step, but we've seen what the coercers are capable of in situations like what happened in Waco and Ruby Ridge. So how can we ensure continuity and maintenance?

Well, the same tactics that creators of digital technology use to make themselves more invulnerable to censorship: decentralization amongst varied jurisdictions.

Instead of just one permanent autonomous zone (P.A.Z.), these PAZs exist all over the world, creating a vetted parallel network of self-liberators – in other words, rebuilding all necessary human institutions upon a framework of Truth and peace.

And while we hope to avoid any of these aforementioned circumstances with the use of privacy/security culture principles, if one "node" in the P.A.Z.NIA network were to go down, the rest should be able to continue without much interruption at all.

This is **The Free Republic of P.A.Z.NIA** (more below) in a nutshell, the first free country in existence, only geographically independent; it certainly is one of those more "grandiose" strategies that Rayo presented in the 1960's, but I think the time is not only now, but the choice to live free in the here and now and NOT implement this strategy has largely dissipated.

Just as when choosing a new vonu home base for strategic relocation, though, if going this route, it's all about location! Do your research and avoid incorporated areas.

At the beginning of 2020, there was some fear and uncertainty. There will always be the uncertainty, but as I examine the world around me, I don't see a more enslaved world with less options…

I see a realm of vast, vast possibilities – not only can we live liberated lifestyles individually, but I truly do believe that we can build the Second Realm.

Hell, we're already doing it.

Chapter 16: (Four Years Later) Rayo's Influence on the Anarchist & Libertarian Communities

In Chapter 2 above, I covered the limited influence Rayo and vonu had on the libertarian community in the 1960's/70's. This mainly consisted of a few notable mentions in old libertarian zines, but for the most part, the man and the strategy largely flew under-the-radar.

Further, Rayo almost undoubtedly influenced Samuel Edward Konkin III in his formulation of agorism, in what he called ethical enclave trading back in the late 1960s. This may be the biggest contribution this mysterious self-liberator had on the community-at-large.

Fast forward to today and it's safe to say that Rayo & vonu are more well-known. Instead of having to define terms every time (as was the case early on in the podcast), self-liberators are adopting the vonu vernacular, and even developing lifestyles and the overarching strategy further — a couple that immediately come to mind are "The Second Realm Notel" episode with JJ and a suggestion by a pseudonymous "John Xina" about solar-powered electric bikes opening up a wildly incredible amount of possibilities for the freethinking freedom seeker.

Many freedom pioneers I know have hit the road as van nomads; more and more are seeing the value of the hardcore security culture vonuans practice, whether the grey man in the physical realm, or crypto-anarchy tactics to guard privacy in the digital.

And **The Vonu Podcast** even got a plug/link from *The Washington Post* after the unfortunate murder of John Galton.

I'm sure there's additional developments, but I'm quite happy with this progress so far.

A few years back, I got in contact with Jim Stumm and was able to conduct an interview with him, "The Man Who Met Rayo." And while Jim only met him once (and ~50 years ago), this insight certainly helped to paint a more vivacious picture of Tom Marshall. Jim was also gracious enough to mail me his entire archive of vonu/libertarian zines from the last 50+ years – at some point, too, expect The Journey of a Self-Liberator (tentative title), with all of Rayo's articles laid out in chronological order.

What will vonu and the realm of self-liberation look like in another four years? The answer to that question largely depends on you.

Chapter 17: (Country Shoppers) The Sovereign Individual is Internationally Flexible

Instead of the scam of political crusading, vote with your feet and partake in some country shopping!

Rayo himself foresaw this opportunity back in the 1960's, and I believe, likely made use of it throughout his journey as a self-liberator. That is, contract engineering jobs where the income was high, and spending/living where the government coercion is low -- he mentioned working in the USSA, and living in tropical island countries in regards to this tactic. He also split time between the US and Canada in his tent & van, making use of the advantages within various jurisdictions.

A few decades later, a book titled **The Sovereign Individual** was published which further highlighted the prospects with the dawning of the computer and Internet age. They argue that "evolutions" in humanity have occurred alongside shifts in the control of violence. And that up until recently, these "deevolutions" have tended to fall on the side of tyranny and collectivism, rather than that of freedom, free will, nature, and a respect for the individual.

Although, in the Information Age, where information, value, and culture are spread freely along wires or through the aether, larger possibilities come into purview, and individual solutions become near certainties.

It's at this juncture that I'd like to introduce the term *internationally flexible* contrasted with *internationally mobile.*

When Rayo used the term, "internationally mobile," it most definitely meant currently living such a perpetually traveling lifestyle. Being internationally flexible, on the other hand, entails having the ability, both legally and practically, to make a quick relocation across jurisdictions, while remaining stationary in dwelling for as long as is possible/desired.

For example, having a converted van with Mexican registration ready-to-go, prepared for the eventuality of having to head for the border. And speaking from experience (direct or indirect, I won't clarify), official Mexican government documentation is not hard to obtain.

For a few hundred dollars, a self-liberator could get a valid Mexican driver's license -- maybe even a Class B chauffeur license which would usually require additional training and certifications here in the USSA. Along with the driver's license, comes a receipt from the local Mexican authority, further verifying the veracity of the ID. And for a decent amount more cost-wise, valid Mexican car registration can be obtained.

At this point, let's walk through a thought experiment (and that's all this is). You have the valid Mexican-issued driver's license and are hoping to obtain, say, a Mexican passport. That's a little more difficult to do all legally and above board. Good news: there are longstanding websites on the Deep Web that offer exactly that, with 99.9% verifiable reputation -- it would cost you $1,200, but this dark market entrepreneur can get you a scannable, authentic-looking Mexican passport to go alongside your REAL, LEGITIMATE, driver's license.

And with a little social engineering skills ("human hacking"), that gives the self-liberator-in-question a really solid footing and access to a second passport/citizenship without all the hassle and time that it would normally take. Of course, this could be replicable in other countries, but I don't know of any offhand. I'd love to hear/share others if that's information you're privy to.

International flexibility being an advantage, this does not mean that public airplanes will be feasible mode of travel for vonuans...they really weren't post-9/11 anyway, but probably not now, and probably not in the future. And with bitcoin's coming future rise, hopefully this voluntary redistribution of wealth will give folks in our network, access to levels of investment capital not previously possible -- this would make private airplanes, decommissioned aircraft carriers, or even a floating hotel in international waters financial potentialities.

Beyond that, international flexibility is made easier when considering the P.A.Z.NIA/Second Realm Network -- see below for more, but in a word, we'll have safe, friendly permanent autonomous zones all over the world!

In a less practical sense, I do see a need for more reports on freedom communities, or otherwise free, safe places. Rayo and Jon Fisher (Jim Stumm) talked about possible countries, uninhabited ocean islands, etc. throughout the 1960's-1980's. It's time for an update, and the P.A.Z.NIA network and coming directory will help in some ways. I've heard good things about Baja, Puerto Vallerta, and a lot of allies exist in central Europe; and I'm pretty confident Acapulco, being the police state it is, is not advised. Beyond that, I've been slacking on my strategic relocation research.

If anyone reading this has insights into any area/location in particular, please do consider reaching out. Written reports would be appreciated, but **The Vonu Podcast** is always an open forum for self-liberators with knowledge to share!

Chapter 18: (Vonu in the Digital World) Digital Privacy, The GhostSystem, & Bitcoin's Role in Liberation

While being a primitive-living hermit, Tom Marshall, the pseudonymous Rayo, was no Luddite when it came to technology. He was a techy electrical engineer, who wrote about encrypted ham radio nets and that payments within ethical enclaves "would most likely be in credits, transmitted thru the net to an 'underground' bank." Despite that, he would probably still be terrified if he were alive to see the digital Babylon that has enshrouded most.

2020 brought forth a lot of 20/20 vision for me, and actually caused me to recoil at technology, pulling back my efforts in the digital realm for probably more than a year. Seeing the "science and technology" on display for the world in the form of Babylon pharmaceutical poisons/geolocation-based track-and-trace (as well as refreshing myself on this multi-centuries old plan vis-a-vis Bill Cooper), I didn't want to have anything to do with it. I was going to dump my smartphone for good, eventually toss the satellite Internet at the homestead, and make some major changes.

That is, until further reflection and developments.

At the present time, there's nothing that "we" can do to stop the progress of technology as it is -- nor do I think that's necessarily "our" place as self-liberators. This digital technology has been a major tool for Second Realm efforts and will continue to be, too...hell, the digital Second Realm is just as much slated for expansion as the physical.

These statements being true, then in the pursuit of self-liberation, "we" must seek to liberate ourselves from these spying-by-default, bot-net seized, insecure devices, and onto our own hardware, loaded with open source, vetted, privacy-hardening software, and eventually, traveling from repeater-to-repeater in our own mesh network. It means that, just as when conducting import-export within the servile society, browsing behaviors and habits must change; you want to blend in at the digital mall, your traffic becoming indistinguishable from the masses, probably through the use of a two-hop VPN, the Tor network, and/or possibilities like i2p or ZeroNet.

Practically speaking, I'm talking about the GhostSystem, hardware hacked by Jamin Biconik. **The GhostSystem** features:

- **GhostPad** for research, communications, and the most private personal data like a private journal
- **GhostPhone** for maximum mobile autonomy
- **GhostBox FreedomBox** for self-hosted services like secure messaging, private search engine, and advanced network wide ad & tracker filtering
- **GhostStation** for gaming and content creation
- **GhostBox Sentinel** network security system with PiAlert and PI-Hole
- **GhostRouter** to secure your network from outside threats
- **GhostVault NAS** to store and serve media
- **GhostStream Entertainment System** as a smart TV replacement
- **GhostEye** surveillance and security system

While there's no perfect solution to the hyper-dynamic Internet, these hardware & software solutions give you essentially the best privacy and security possible, especially at this user-friendliness level. Please note, this is all free-and-open source software, so you can install all these on your own hardware; but soon, Jamin will eventually offer the entire GhostSystem for those like me who want the hard work done for them. This can all understandably seem overwhelming, but this is what needs to be done. "We" must own our shit and start building out our own secure infrastructure.

Beyond that, plans are in the works to build out our own, trusted, vetted, and decentralized Tor/VPN network, which will mitigate some of the riskiest hurdles of Tor, i.e. hijacked exit nodes, likely operated by the NSA.

This brings forth the liberating potentialities of bitcoin (BTC), especially when paired with a similar mindset. Running a full node and becoming proficient with software implementations like non-custodial CoinJoins make on-chain privacy an actual reality.

For me, I'm striving to bring all my actions in alignment with my principles, and using fraudulent government fiat currency as little as possible is the objective. These above privacy innovations and ease-of-spending bitcoin (i.e. no-KYC bitcoin debit cards that work anywhere Visa is accepted, gift cards for any place you could desire to spend money, etc.) solidify one of bitcoin's features of enabling a self-liberator to totally route around First Realm institutions.

Earn bitcoin > coinjoin bitcoin > spend bitcoin > save bitcoin. It's truly a beautiful cycle.

In conclusion, my preference would honestly be to toss out most of my digital devices and work towards a minimalist digital lifestyle. Unfortunately, I don't see that as being totally possible...but what I do see as possible is using these tools in a self-liberating capacity to advance the Second Realm for as long as they're feasible. And when things begin to look untenable, as adaptive self-liberators, "we" will change our lifestyle again and again to achieve our goals.

Chapter 19: (The Free Republic of P.A.Z.NIA) A Network of Ethical Enclaves

The Model Country

Back in the mid-20th century, libertarian new country pioneer, Erwin S. Strauss (who is STILL around, and who still runs *The [Libertarian] Connection*), wrote about the idea of a model country in his book, *How to Start Your Own Country*. Therein, he posits:

"Many find it a rewarding hobby to run a model railroad, or operate model airplanes. These model enterprises have all the trappings of the real thing, in miniature. Similarly, it's possible to run a 'model country.' You need only declare your home to be an independent nation, and proceed from there."

The Free Republic of P.A.Z.NIA is the newest iteration of this concept, our mission of truly founding the first free country. The flagship is Veritas, but other nodes in the P.A.Z.NIA network will serve as "cities," scattered all over the world. More importantly, considering the coercive nature of our world, this decentralized, security culture-minded approach (and the already rather large digital community of freedom seekers) all but guarantee the success of the network, so long as resources, time, and concentration are given to it —

in other words, as long as we continue to utilize our generative force of creation to build the Second Realm; to manifest Eden.

As I outlined above, Spring 2020 was a major catalyst for change. In addition to taking strides towards my own self-sufficiency, I decided to try and host a freedom festival at the homestead, naturally called VONUFEST.

Before long, I was declaring my 22-acre homestead to be independent from the United Soviet States of America, modifying a Constitution, and officially launching reputable departments such as the P.A.Z.NIA Department of Freedom, The P.A.Z.NIA Secret Space Program, and much more.

In September 2020 (Year 0 on our calendar), 20 or 30 self-liberators made it out to experience P.A.Z.NIA and for our Rebirth of Freedom ceremony, wherein we signed the P.A.Z.NIA Constitution and I gave a bit of a speech. It was quite a spectacular event.

The short history behind us, what is P.A.Z.NIA?

The Free Republic of P.A.Z.NIA is a "new country project", only unlike others, P.A.Z.NIA is geographically independent. Nodes ("cities") consist of self-sufficient homesteads, van nomad city squat spots, wilderness camping, or whatever other areas are on offer from vetted P.A.Z.NIANs.

The other stark difference from many "countries" is that P.A.Z.NIA is founded upon security culture principles, which means that pseudonyms are encouraged and that all visitors & network participants must be vetted[*] ([*]except for unvetted areas like The P.A.Z.NIA Seed Exchange).

As mentioned above, the goal is to build a parallel society, the rebuilding of all necessary human institutions. This obviously necessitates the founding of various departments to handle such tasks:

- Department of Freedom (passports, ID's, Constitution)
- P.A.Z.NIA Secret Space Program (investigations into breakthrough, independent energy)
- Department of Transportation (the home of our coming decentralized logistics network)
- The Great P.A.Z.NIA Seed Exchange
- Department of Tourism (for off-site travel to areas around Little Egypt)

- Department of Bitcoin (P.A.Z.NIA General Bitcoin Fund & Coming P.A.Z.NIA Bitcoin Mines)
- Department of Health & Wellness
- P.A.Z.NIA Free Press
- The P.A.Z.NIA Library
- The P.A.Z.NIA Apothecary

In addition to self-liberation and self-sufficiency, we also host numerous gatherings throughout the year, to give folks a chance to experience Second Realm culture. Yearly events include:

- July 4th Weekend (Anarchy Day Weekend)
- Labor Day Weekend (Agorism Day Weekend)
- Thanksgiving (Dabsgiving/Ethical Enclave Day)

Additional, unofficial events are hosted throughout the year – stay up-to-date by joining the P.A.Z.NIA Committee of Correspondence chat or check out the VONUFEST tab at PAZNIA.com.

Anyone can help support & join this Second Realm Network by becoming an HONORARY STEAKholder. Vetted self-liberators can become FOUNDING STEAKholders, reaping even more benefits of this network in physical space & time.

We're still early on in this vision, but long-term, we hope to have a thriving, large network of P.A.Z.NIAs around the world, with our own accompanying independent logistics & delivery network.

We will provide all our own necessities of life (this division of labor being divided across the network), and for items/services needed from the First Realm, will utilize proxy merchants as necessary…

But the end goal is minimal interaction with the society founded upon coercion, and maximal love & community with those vibrating on the same frequency.

If you're interested in joining the Second Realm, just visit PAZNIA.com. Cheers from *#TheFreeRepublic*!

Additional Resources

- **The Vonu Podcast**: If you want to learn more about anything covered in this book, I'd highly recommend you check out the podcast Kyle Rearden and I do. In season 1, we covered the philosophy of vonu, season 2 was the practice of vonu, and the current season, 3, is where we develop and update vonu to the modern day.
    - www.vonupodcast.com
- **Vonu: The Search for Personal Freedom, Number 2 – Letters from Rayo**
    - www.vonupodcast.com/vonu2
- **Vonulife, March 1973 (Special Edition)**
    - www.vonupodcast.com/vl
- **Ocean Freedom Notes**
    - www.vonupodcast.com/ofn
- **Self-Liberation Notes**
    - www.vonupodcast.com/sln
- **Going Mobile**
    - www.vonupodcast.com/gm
- **Low-Cost Living**
    - www.vonupodcast.com/lcl
- **Dwelling Portably [sic]**
    - www.vonupodcast.com/dp
- **Articles About Vonu**
    - www.vonupodcast.com/vonuarticles
- **Liberty Under Attack**: If you're seeking out paths to personal freedom, then you need to check out The Freedom Umbrella of Direct Action and the Direct Action Series.
    - www.libertyunderattack.com/FUDA
    - www.libertyunderattack.com/DAS
- **The Last Bastille Blog**: This is Kyle's blog and it's chockfull of incredible, highly valuable information. He has written over

150 book reviews, a couple books pertinent to vonu, and much more.

- o www.thelastbastille.com

- **YouTube**: If you're pursuing any of the lifestyle changes or strategies I covered above, then YouTube will be your best friend. Recommended search terms: "van dwelling," "living aboard a boat," "minimalist sailboating," etc.

About The Author

Shane started ***Liberty Under Attack*** in mid-2012 when he was just beginning his research into the nature of reality. He began with an adventure down the conspiratorial rabbit hole for a while, focusing primarily on the work of the late Milton William ("Bill") Cooper.

In February 2015, Shane started ***LUA Radio***, which was one of his goals for quite a long time, and would prove to be the most critical step in his development personally, as well as the point of origination for the now-real world connections in the Second Realm.

Not long after launching LUA Radio, he found the philosophies of voluntaryism/free market anarchism, and then shifted his focus towards solutions to increase personal freedom in the here and now.

As a next logical step, in January 2017, he launched ***The Vonu Podcast*** with Kyle Rearden, a podcast dedicated to promoting the philosophy of vonu and developing the liberating strategy up into the modern day.

This was about the time he began writing his first book, ***Vonu: A Strategy for Self-Liberation***, and founded his publishing outfit, ***Liberty Under Attack Publications***, which focuses on strategies and tactics for self-liberation, in addition to anarchist/agorist fiction.

He currently resides on his 22-acre homestead in ***The Free Republic of P.A.Z.NIA*** raising his lambs, goats, and chickens, & publishing books and podcasts. He hopes to publish more of his own works soon (too many unfinished works-in-progress!).

Contact Shane:
- Email: shane@libertyunderattack.com
- Email: coordinator@paznia.com
- Telegram: @LibertyUnderAttack

Edited By: TJ Connolly, Aga Franks, Jeremy Henggeler, and Jason Boothe

Thank you for your service!

LIBERTY UNDER ATTACK PUBLICATIONS *tell your story*

1. **An Illusive Phantom of Hope: A Critique of Reformism** by Kyle Rearden (Audiobook/Anthology)
2. **The Production of Security** by Gustave de Molinari (Audiobook)
3. **Are Cops Constitutional?** by Roger Roots (Audiobook)
4. **Argumentation Ethics: An Anthology** by Hans-Herman Hoppe et al (Anthology)
5. **Just Below The Surface: A Guide to Security Culture** by Kyle Rearden (Audiobook/Paperback)
6. **Sedition, Subversion, and Sabotage, Field Manual No. 1: A Three Part Solution to the State** by Ben Stone (Paperback/Audiobook)
7. **#agora** by anonymous (Paperback/Audiobook)
8. **Vonu: A Strategy for Self-Liberation** by Shane Radliff (Paperback)
9. **Second Realm: Book on Strategy** by Smuggler and XYZ (Paperback/Audiobook)
10. **Vonu: The Search for Personal Freedom** by Rayo (Special Paperback Reprint/Audiobook)
11. **Vonu: The Search for Personal Freedom, Part 2 [Letters From Rayo]** (Paperback)
12. **Going Mobile** by Tom Marshall (Paperback/Audiobook)
13. **Anarchist to Abolitionist: A Bad Quaker's Journey** by Ben Stone
14. **Brushfire, A Thriller** by Matthew Wojtecki (Paperback/Audiobook)
15. **2048 (A BRUSHFIRE THRILLER)** by Matthew Wojtecki
16. **VonuLife, March 1973** by Rayo et al (Paperback)
17. **Ocean Freedom Notes** by Jim Stumm, Rayo, et al (Paperback)
18. **The Big Book of Secret Hiding Places** by Jack Luger (Paperback)
19. **The Invention of Evil** by Henry Jones (Paperback/Kindle)
20. **Low Cost Living Notes** by Jim Stumm et al (Paperback/Kindle)
21. **Survival Gardening Notes** by Jim Stumm et al (Paperback/Kindle)
22. **The Permanent Floating Voluntary Society** by Kerry Thornley (Paperback/Kindle)
23. **A Vonu Guide to Firearms** by Josiah Warren & Shane Radliff (Paperback)

Visit <u>LibertyUnderAttack.com</u> for discounted bundles, privacy tools, and more!

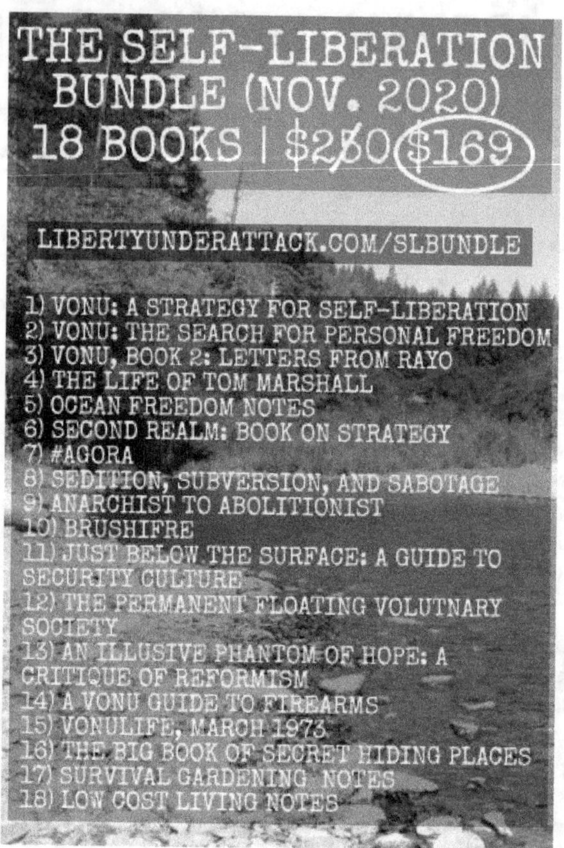
THE SELF-LIBERATION BUNDLE (NOV. 2020)
18 BOOKS | $250 $169
LIBERTYUNDERATTACK.COM/SLBUNDLE
1) VONU: A STRATEGY FOR SELF-LIBERATION
2) VONU: THE SEARCH FOR PERSONAL FREEDOM
3) VONU, BOOK 2: LETTERS FROM RAYO
4) THE LIFE OF TOM MARSHALL
5) OCEAN FREEDOM NOTES
6) SECOND REALM: BOOK ON STRATEGY
7) #AGORA
8) SEDITION, SUBVERSION, AND SABOTAGE
9) ANARCHIST TO ABOLITIONIST
10) BRUSHFIRE
11) JUST BELOW THE SURFACE: A GUIDE TO SECURITY CULTURE
12) THE PERMANENT FLOATING VOLUTNARY SOCIETY
13) AN ILLUSIVE PHANTOM OF HOPE: A CRITIQUE OF REFORMISM
14) A VONU GUIDE TO FIREARMS
15) VONULIFE, MARCH 1973
16) THE BIG BOOK OF SECRET HIDING PLACES
17) SURVIVAL GARDENING NOTES
18) LOW COST LIVING NOTES

BOOKS & PRIVACY TOOLS AVAILABLE
CALYXOS
[GhostPads Coming Soon]
LIBERTY UNDER ATTACK PUBLICATIONS
LIBERTYUNDERATTACK.COM
Share your story, find your freedom.
LIBERTYUNDERATTACK.COM/PrivacyTools